American Presidents

A Very Peculiar History®

'Anyone who is capable of getting themselves
made President should on no account be
allowed to do the job.'

Douglas Adams
The Hitchhiker's Guide to the Galaxy

For Roger W. Baker,
my old buddy across the Pond

DA

Editor: Nick Pierce
Artist: David Lyttleton
Additional artwork: Shutterstock

Published in Great Britain in MMXX by
Book House, an imprint of
The Salariya Book Company Ltd
25 Marlborough Place, Brighton BN1 1UB
www.salariya.com

ISBN: 978-1-912904-21-1

SALARIYA

SCRIBO BOOK HOUSE SCRIBBLERS

1 3 5 7 9 8 6 4 2

A CIP catalogue record for this book is available
from the British Library.

Printed and bound in China.
Printed on paper from sustainable sources.

Visit
www.salariya.com
for our online catalogue and
free fun stuff.

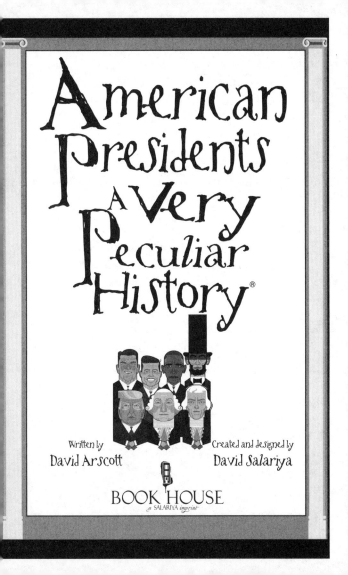

American Presidents

A Very Peculiar History®

Written by
David Arscott

Created and designed by
David Salariya

BOOK HOUSE
a SALARIYA imprint

'Nearly all men can stand adversity,
but if you want to test a man's character
give him power.'
Abraham Lincoln

'No president who performs his
duties faithfully and conscientiously
can have any leisure.'
James Knox Polk

'The most successful politician is he
who says what the people are thinking
most often in the loudest voice.'
Theodore Roosevelt

'A sense of humour is part of the act of
leadership, of getting along with people,
of getting things done.'
Dwight D. Eisenhower

'It's not *doing* what is right that's hard
for a President. It's *knowing* what is
right.'
Lyndon B. Johnson

Contents

'
Hail to the Chief who in triumph advances! Honoured and blessed be the evergreen Pine!
'

HAIL
TO THE CHIEF

Among the many differences between the first US president, who according to legend couldn't bring himself to tell a lie, and the 45th, forever wielding a hatchet against inconvenient 'fake news', none is more striking than their relative spheres of influence.

George Washington, while setting standards all future presidents would feel obliged to acknowledge, commanded a small and fragile union of former British colonies. Rather more than two centuries later Donald Trump could, in his less shy moments, claim to be the most powerful man in the world.

Ruffles and flourishes

One little perk of being top honcho is to have a military band serenade you on official occasions with the jaunty 'Hail to the Chief', the presidential anthem, preceding it with an honorary fanfare of four ruffles (on the drums) and flourishes (bugles).

The choral version has words from Sir Walter Scott's The Lady of the Lake, set to music around 1812 by the Englishman James Sanderson:

Hail to the Chief who in triumph advances!
Honored and blessed be the evergreen Pine!

Although most presidents have liked it, Chester A. Arthur was an exception. In the 1880s he did the patriotic thing and had John Philip Sousa (leader of the United States Marine Band and famous for his military marches) compose a 'Presidential Polonaise' to take its place at indoor events and 'Semper Fidelis' for those in the open air.

Sousa's reputation was not enough: 'Hail to the Chief' soon made a comeback, and it became the official presidential anthem under Harry Truman after the Second World War.

This status may be disputed,* but the amazing thing is that almost any American can aspire to rule over this vibrant nation of more than 300 million people, strut the international stage and have a finger on the nuclear button. True, it helps to have access to a few million dollars at election time, but otherwise there's not much standing in your way.

You must be a 'natural-born' citizen of the USA – but it's OK to have been born abroad as long as your parents are American citizens

You have to be at least 35 years old, which does mean a bit of a wait if you're a teenage hopeful

You need to have been resident in the country for 14 years

The immense personal clout of the president derives largely, of course, from the heft of the United States on the world stage, but the Constitution gives the incumbent impressive powers domestically too.

* As Forbes Magazine has done: in its 2018 rankings the US president featured third behind Xi Jinping of China and Russia's Vladimir Putin.

Here are a few of the perks of the job for a POTUS*:

- In the role of Commander-in-Chief, he (perhaps one day she, but never yet) can deploy the armed forces in battle. Declaring war is actually the job of Congress, but the president has 60 days before he needs to get his bold adventure rubber-stamped, and (e.g. Korea, Vietnam) that's never been a problem

- He can grant reprieves for federal offences – except for impeachment, which might mean pardoning himself

- Through 'executive orders' he can bypass Congress to issue legally binding rules and regulations to federal agencies – although they can be overturned if deemed unconstitutional

- He can veto legislation, which then has to go back to Congress and receive two-thirds of the vote in each house if it's to survive

* The ugly, but unavoidable, acronym for President of the United States. Similarly FLOTUS for the First Lady and SCOTUS for the Supreme Court.

Checks and balances

A key principle of the Constitution is that the power of the executive (that is, the president, his cabinet and the federal agencies) should be tempered by the legislature (the law-making Senate and House of Representatives) and the judiciary (the Supreme Court and other federal courts). It's great in theory!

The Strangelove question

In Stanley Kubrick's satire *Dr Strangelove* the US president tries to prevent an unhinged Air Force general pitching the world into nuclear war, but the film inevitably raises the spectre of an unstable president himself pushing the nuclear button – and the question of what could stop him.

The answer isn't comforting. The 60-day rule (facing page) was designed to allow a rapid response to events, and it means that Congress has no immediate power to control an impulsive president. All that could stop him would be the refusal of his subordinates to carry out his orders.

Presidential facts 'n' figures

Youngest at his inauguration: Theodore Roosevelt, 42 years and 322 days
Oldest: Donald Trump, 70 years and 220 days

Longest-serving: Franklin D. Roosevelt, 4,422 days
Shortest-serving: William Henry Harrison, 32 days

Tallest: Abraham Lincoln, 193cm (6ft 4in)
Shortest: James Madison, 163cm (5ft 4in)

Heaviest: William Taft, 325 pounds (23.2 stone)
Lightest: James Madison, 100 pounds (7.1 stone)

Had most children: John Tyler, 15
Had most wives: Donald Trump, 3
Never married: James Buchanan

Grandfather/grandson: William Henry Harrison, Benjamin Harrison
Fifth cousins: Theodore Roosevelt, Franklin D. Roosevelt

States where most presidents were born: Virginia, 8; Ohio, 7

In practice, a domineering president can get away with a great deal. As we've seen, he can veto legislation arriving on his desk from Congress, and as his political party is almost certain to be well represented in both houses it's unlikely that his opponents will garner enough votes to thwart him.

As for the legal check, it's a striking feature of the US system that the president appoints judges to the Supreme Court. It's in his interest to find a candidate likely to interpret the law as best suits him, with either a conservative or a liberal bent. His choice does have to be approved by the Senate, but unless the nominee is blatantly unsuitable, he's very likely to get his way.

The bully pulpit

And then there's so-called 'soft power' – the influence a president has simply by being guaranteed an audience. Theodore Roosevelt, who had a tendency to play the preacher with his ideas about civility and social justice, referred to this exalted position as his 'bully pulpit'.

As if enjoying the wielding of so much power isn't enough, the president gets a pretty decent annual remuneration:

> Salary $400,000
> Expenses $50,000
> Non-taxable travel allowance $100,000
> Entertainment $19,000

The West Wing

A fascination with presidential politics gave Aaron Sorkin's TV series *The West Wing* cult status after it was first broadcast on NBC in 2006. Set in the West Wing of the White House, it featured the fictitious Democrat president Josiah Bartlet, played by Martin Sheen, and eventually ran for seven seasons.

The plot lines echoed real events of the time. Although some rightwing critics thought it too soft on its liberal characters (and Gerald Ford's daughter Susan said she couldn't watch it because 'they turn left and right where you're not supposed to'), it was praised by political science professors, former White House staffers and even that redoubtable elder statesman Henry Kissinger.

When the game's over there's a yearly pension equivalent to the salary of a current cabinet member (more than $200,000, since you're asking), plus payroll for office staff, free postage for life and a host of other benefits which probably double that figure. Oh, and the state pays for the personal protection of each ex-president and his family.

Take a deep breath: the amount splashed out on former White House occupants amounts to millions of dollars a year.

Red or blue

What any presidential hopeful needs is money (sorry to go on about it, but the Trump/Clinton contest in 2016 ran up bills of $2.65 billion, or £2 billion) and the backing of one of the major parties – not a legal necessity, but unless you're a Republican (red) or a Democrat (blue) you don't really stand a chance.

The third indispensable requirement is the energy to take you through an exhaustive round of devil-take-the-hindmost 'primaries' in the months before the national election itself.

> 'Every election is a sort of advance
> auction sale of stolen goods.'
>
> *H.L. Mencken*

These primaries (and there are caucuses, too, but let's not quibble) are the laborious way the parties decide who will represent them when polling day comes around. The rules vary between the parties and from state to state, but the upshot is that the admirable and despicable characteristics of every wannabe are given full public scrutiny for month after wearying month until the less attractive (or so everyone fondly hopes) are gradually, and brutally, winnowed out.

It's not a spectacle for the faint-hearted!

Change and no change

Americans are notoriously fond of plain speaking, and when they talk about the presidential elections that's exactly what they mean: they're voting for a new (sometimes the serving) president and his deputy – and that's quite enough for one busy day, thank you.

The White House

The Irishman James Hoban designed the president's neo-classical official residence (located at 1600 Pennsylvania Avenue NW, Washington DC, should you think of posting a letter), although it's seen plenty of changes since John Adams first occupied it in 1800.

Within a year Thomas Jefferson had moved in and, with the architect Benjamin Latrobe, added colonnades on each wing for stables and storage. The British set the building ablaze in 1814 (*page 56*), and the south and north porticoes were added after its restoration.

In 1901 Theodore Roosevelt added the famous West Wing. (William Taft would create the first Oval Office in it eight years later.) His smaller East Wing was expanded in 1942, covering the underground bunker which is now known as the Presidential Emergency Operations Center.

A major reconstruction took place in 1948, when the load-bearing walls were found to be close to failure. Today it's a National Heritage Site and has been voted second on a list of 'America's Favorite Architecture' – beaten to the top spot by the Empire State Building.

Here's a rough-and-ready guide to how two western democracies go very different ways about organising their elections.

In the UK all parliamentary seats are up for grabs at the same time at a general election. Voters choose from a raft of local candidates representing parties great and small, and when it's all over either Labour or the Conservatives (in recent times) has a majority big enough to run the country. The leader of the winning party becomes Prime Minister.

In the US it isn't like that at all. Congress is made up of the Senate (two senators for each state) and the House of Representatives (well over four hundred of them), and each house has its own election cycle totally independent of the presidential shenanigans.

This means not only that their political make-up is unaffected by the race to the White House, but that a new president may find him/herself faced by a Congress dominated by the opposition.

Thank heavens for vetoes and the bully pulpit!

Proxy voting

A strange element of the US system to an outsider is that votes don't go directly to the candidates but to members of the Electoral College – their number reflecting how many members each state sends to congress. These 'electors' are entrusted to honour the popular vote, in most states on a winner-takes-all basis.

Hanging chads

The most dramatic end to a presidential race in modern times occurred in 2000, when the parties were neck-and-neck and everything depended on the result in Florida. George W. Bush had a lead of just 327 votes over Vice President Al Gore in a poll of 6 million, but in some areas punched card machines had been used, and there were many failures, leaving the confetti-like 'chads' not fully released. Gore demanded manual recounts in four 'hanging chad' counties, but only three had been completed before a deadline imposed by Florida's Secretary of State. Bush was declared the winner – and thereby squeezed home as President. The rest is history ...

A peep at the Veep

John Adams, the very first American vice president, lamented having the 'most insignificant' job imaginable – and although the role eventually became busier, it wasn't until 1961 that the No. 2 was given an office in the White House.

Known variously as VPOTUS, VP and Veep, the vice president (salary $230,700) is President of the Senate, with a casting vote to break a tie, but much of his back-up legislative work goes unseen.

Just ponder, though, what the following have in common: John Tyler, Millard Fillimore, Andrew Johnson, Chester A. Arthur, Theodore Roosevelt, Calvin Coolidge, Harry S. Truman, Lyndon B. Johnson, Gerald Ford.

Yes, they all stepped up to the plate mid-term to take over the presidency itself.

And these: John Adams, George Bush, Thomas Jefferson, Martin Van Buren, Richard Nixon.

They all served as Veep before being elected to the presidency in their own right.

They nearly always do – although the term 'faithless elector' has been coined for the very occasional bad apple.

Some six weeks later these 'electors' convene in their state capitals to pledge their vote for the president and vice president, and during the first week of the following January the results are at last opened and declared at a joint session of Congress. Job done!

Does the system work? Only four times in US history has a president won an election despite losing the overall popular vote – the last two being George W. Bush and Donald Trump.

And are such 'minority' presidents abashed? Think 'war on terror', think aggressive tweeting. Only the driven reach the White House, and once inside the Oval Office they're hellbent on their mission, for good or ill.

We'll let you judge the good and ill in the pages that follow. It's safe to say that there have been saints and sinners, high achievers and abject failures, the wise and the foolish. Fortunately for us, most of them have also been pretty entertaining . . .

List of American Presidents

A popular pub question asks 'How many American presidents have there been?' The catch is that Grover Cleveland served twice but not consecutively – so that when Donald Trump became the 45th president, he was only the 44th man to have held the post.

1 George Washington, 1789–1797
2 John Adams, 1797–1801
3 Thomas Jefferson, 1801–1809
4 James Madison, 1809–1817
5 James Monroe, 1817–1825
6 John Quincy Adams, 1825–1829
7 Andrew Jackson, 1829–1837
8 Martin Van Buren, 1837–1841
9 William Henry Harrison, 1841
10 John Tyler, 1841–1845
11 James K. Polk, 1845–1849
12 Zachary Taylor, 1849–1850
13 Millard Fillmore, 1850–1853
14 Franklin Pierce, 1853–1857
15 James Buchanan, 1857–1861
16 Abraham Lincoln, 1861–1865
17 Andrew Johnson, 1865–1869
18 Ulysses S. Grant, 1869–1877

19 Rutherford B. Hayes, 1877–1881
20 James A. Garfield, 1881
21 Chester A. Arthur, 1881–1885
22 Grover Cleveland, 1885–1889
23 Benjamin Harrison, 1889–1893
24 Grover Cleveland, 1893–1897
25 William McKinley, 1897–1901
26 Theodore Roosevelt, 1901–1909
27 William Howard Taft, 1909–1913
28 Woodrow Wilson, 1913–1921
29 Warren G. Harding, 1921–1923
30 Calvin Coolidge, 1923–1929
31 Herbert Hoover, 1929–1933
32 Franklin Delano Roosevelt, 1933–1945
33 Harry S. Truman, 1945–1953
34 Dwight D. Eisenhower, 1953–1961
35 John F. Kennedy, 1961–1963
36 Lyndon B. Johnson, 1963–1969
37 Richard Nixon, 1969–1974
38 Gerald Ford, 1974–1977
39 Jimmy Carter, 1977–1981
40 Ronald Reagan, 1981–1989
41 George H.W. Bush, 1989–1993
42 Bill Clinton, 1993–2001
43 George W. Bush, 2001–2009
44 Barack Obama, 2009–2017
45 Donald Trump, 2017–

‘ a dangerous man,
and one who ought
not be trusted
with the reins of
government ’

fOUNDING fATHERS

I magine being given your very own brand new nation to run, with a blank page on which to pen its defining constitution: first you feel the exhilaration of harnessing all your dreams and experience in pursuit of the common good, but very soon you're likely to quake at the awesome responsibilities and expectations thrust upon you.

The United States was lucky in the quality of the men who first shaped it, but they argued violently among themselves about how best to marry the often conflicting aspirations of strong government and individual freedom, of federation and state independence.

Upstaging Washington

If you really want to annoy devotees of George Washington all you have to do is tell them that he wasn't really the first president of the United States at all – which is true up to a point.

In 1781, before the present Constitution was drawn up, the thirteen states came together under Articles of Confederation. It was a loose alliance, though, and because the colonists had shed their blood in defeating a monarchy and thus had an understandable fear of putting too much power in one man's hands, their (unpaid) president wasn't given much more to do than chair meetings and sign off congressional documents.

But with that huge caveat, let's acknowledge John Hanson of Maryland as the very first president of that special kind, and add the names of the seven who followed him for a year at a time before Washington trod the boards as the genuine article: Elias Boudinot, Thomas Mifflin, Richard Henry Lee, John Hancock, Nathaniel Gorham, Arthur St Clair and Cyrus Griffin.

Back in 1973 the historian Richard B. Morris drew up a short-list of seven eminent leaders of the American Revolution against British rule worthy of being acclaimed Founding Fathers of the new independent nation:

> John Adams
> Benjamin Franklin
> Alexander Hamilton
> John Jay
> Thomas Jefferson
> James Madison
> George Washington

These strong characters played various roles in negotiating the end of the revolutionary war, drafting the Constitution and running the first American government, but four of them also served as the early presidents and therefore earn a special mention here.

farmer George

The greatest of them all was **George Washington** (1732–1799), who thought of himself as a farmer and eventually retired with relief to his Mount Vernon estate on the banks of the Potomac in Virginia – but only after years of varied and exhausting public service.

His chief theme as president was the need for the states to work together rather than each to fight its own corner,* having learned the hard way while serving (unpaid, at his own insistence) as commander-in-chief of the Continental Army against the British.

This was a rag-taggle force, because the individual states were disinclined to put up enough money to finance it. The men were badly paid, poorly equipped, ill-fed and thus prone to sickness, while even the officers sent to him (many 'from the lowest class of the people', he complained) often proved cowardly, became deserters or plundered the local inhabitants. There were several mutinies, too.

A mild, devout but pragmatic man, Washington had the worst offenders flogged – up to 500 lashes – and he even introduced a 12m (40ft) gallows, prepared 'to hang two or three on it, as an example to others'.

---

* He was opposed to the creation of political parties, because he thought they encouraged a factional selfishness, but he was the only president who was ever elected without being affiliated to one of them.

He also faced a revolt by the Conway Cabal, a group of senior army officers who wanted him removed. It came to nothing, but any military leader will sympathise with a letter he wrote in response to the endless sniping he suffered:

It is a much easier and less distressing thing to draw remonstrances in a comfortable room by a good fireside than to occupy a cold, bleak hill, and sleep under frost and snow, without clothes or blankets.

Mr President

The decisive battle came at Yorktown in October 1781, and once the terms of the British surrender had been agreed Washington stood down – anxious, as a staunch Republican, that power in the fledgling nation should rest with Congress rather than a garlanded military man.

He was a reluctant politician, too, but in the febrile atmosphere of the time – there was even an armed revolt (Shays' Rebellion) by agricultural workers in Massachussets – he felt obliged to throw his weight behind the argument for a strong federal government.

Washington had feared that, thanks to the reluctance of individual states to yield any of their sovereignty, the Union would be held together by nothing but 'a rope of sand'. In the event his influence lead to the wording of a Constitution much to his liking – and, in 1789, to his election (with a majority in every state) as the first president of the United States.

His inauguration was suitably grand, with a marching band and a 13-gun salute, but the man himself was typically modest and mindful of setting an example for future generations.

- Rather than strut his stuff in military uniform, he appeared for the occasion in a suit of simple broadcloth

- Offered a range of highfalutin titles such as His Highness the President of the United States, he asked to be addressed simply as Mr President – a convention that has lasted to this day

- He said he wanted to do the job for expenses only – but Congress overruled him and set a fixed salary, which he accepted

Tensions

In appointing his first cabinet, Washington knew that feathers would fly. Not only were his secretary of state Thomas Jefferson and his treasury secretary Alexander Hamilton from opposing parties, but both were strong and implacable.

'Hamilton and myself were daily pitted in the cabinet like two cocks,' Jefferson wrote later.

That cherry tree ...

It was the episcopalian minister Mason Locke Weems who first recounted the legend of the six-year-old George confessing to damaging one of his father's cherry trees: 'I cannot tell a lie! I did cut it with my little hatchet.'

His *Life of George Washington* was an instant hit when published in 1800, but – curiously – it wasn't until the fifth edition six years later that Parson Weems introduced the morally uplifting cherry tree tale.

Saved by the musical!

The faces of early presidents grace most of the commonly used dollar bills:

> $1 George Washington
> $2 Thomas Jefferson
> $5 Abraham Lincoln
> $20 Andrew Jackson
> $50 Ulysses S. Grant
> $100 Benjamin Franklin

The exception is the $10 bill, which honours Alexander Hamilton. When the Treasury Department decided that the black activist Harriet Tubman should be represented on a note from 2020 to celebrate the centenary of women getting the vote, Washington's treasury secretary was singled out for the chop – until a very strange thing happened.

Hamilton, a rapped-through musical based on the founding father's rather racy life, took Broadway by storm and won a host of awards, including the 2016 Pulitzer drama prize.

It was suddenly a bad idea to displace him. Tubman looked set to demote Jackson to the reverse of the $20 bill instead – until Donald Trump (a Jackson devotee) denounced the whole idea as 'pure political correctness'.

Their first major row was over the creation of a national bank. Hamilton, a Federalist, argued that the institution would settle war debts, support a single currency and boost the economy. Jefferson, a republican, fought any centralising power that might lead to tyranny.

Washington eventually backed Hamilton, but the fragility of the newly minted democracy persisted throughout his first presidency and was instrumental in persuading him to serve a second term.

The Whiskey Rebellion

Just as the British imposing 'taxation without representation' had fuelled the American Revolution, so in 1791 the very first 'taxation without *local* representation' by the new federal government sparked a violent uprising in Western Pennsylvania.

Imposed on distilled spirits in general, this came down particularly hard on farmers accustomed to turning their surplus grain into whiskey – not only for cash sales, but often as a medium of exchange.

Things came to a head in 1794, when a marshal arrived to serve writs on those distillers who had refused to pay. More than five hundred armed men attacked the (fortified) home of a tax inspector, and the upshot was that Washington himself led an army of 13,000 men to suppress the insurgency.

Trouble with France

Meanwhile the French had staged their own revolution, and during the decade from 1789 the United States was close to being drawn into the war between Britain and France.

Once again Hamilton and Jefferson were at loggerheads, the former in favour of closer ties with the Old Country and the latter, supporting France, fearing an undercutting of republicanism.

As with the national bank controversy, Washington gave the nod to Hamilton. The Jay Treaty of 1795 (ratified by the Senate with a two-thirds majority) forged a new relationship with Britain – although this fierce political argument would rumble on for years.

An angry radical

The English radical writer Thomas Paine (1737–1809) was a promoter of both the American and French revolutions. He met Benjamin Franklin in London in 1774, later moved to Philadelphia and wrote the pamphlet *Common Sense*, which denounced the British monarchy as tyrannical.

George Washington, who took inspiration from his writing, ordered his officers to read Paine's *The American Crisis* to the army before his famous crossing of the Delaware before victory at Trenton in 1776.

After returning to Britain, Paine wrote the celebrated *Rights of Man*, fled to France after being charged with treason and was elected a member of the National Assembly. Thrown into jail for opposing Louis XVI's execution, he claimed life-saving American citizenship but was refused.

Although the American ambassador to France, James Monroe, eventually secured his release, an embittered Paine wrote a virulent open letter to Washington, accusing him of promoting policies which betrayed the principles of the American Revolution.

Washington retired gratefully to his Mount Vernon plantation in 1797, declaring that he was about to experience 'more enjoyment than in all the business with which I have been occupied for upwards of forty years'.

In truth the place was somewhat run-down through neglect. He had to sell off tracts of land to settle his debts – and he was to play the gentleman farmer for less than three years.

The long farewell

Washington's farewell address, expressing his political credo, written in the florid style of the time and running to 7,641 words and 32-handwritten pages, lives on to this day.

On his birthday each February a member of the Senate reads the whole thing out during a legislative session: the speediest reading to date came in at 39 minutes, while the most deliberate took 68 minutes.

After this marathon the senator writes his or her name in a leather-bound book and makes a brief personal remark about the address and its impact.

In December 1799, a vigorous 67-year-old*
happily managing his remaining estate and
socialising with friends, former colleagues and
lionising visitors, he was struck down by an
infection of the epiglottis. He was dead within
a day of falling ill.

*Like many men in his position, Washington
kept slaves – more than a hundred of them. In
his will he expressed his dislike of the system and
(the only Founding Father to do so) granted them
their freedom.*

Second string

Pity the man who had to follow in the footsteps
of the 'Father of the Nation'. It's not that **John
Adams** (1735–1826) was unprepared for the
job – he was a leading political theorist, he'd
helped draft the Declaration of Independence,
he'd negotiated the Treaty of Paris which
settled the terms of the British surrender and
he'd been Washington's vice president for a
full eight years.

** Although he had lost all his teeth. His dentures were a wired-up
assemblage of hippopotamus ivory and teeth extracted from other people
– possibly his own slaves.*

No, he was simply dealt a bad hand and lacked his predecessor's supreme authority.

The electoral system of the time awarded the vice presidency to whoever came second in the poll. Adams, who had had to fight off a challenge from Alexander Hamilton for the Federalist Party nomination, scraped home by two votes ahead of the Democrat-Republican leader Thomas Jefferson, and the two were shackled together for the next four years. (This potentially fraught cross-party pairing would never be repeated.)

Fortunately they were friends,* and the new Veep busied himself with party political rather than governmental affairs.

Worse for Adams was the divide within his own party. Three of his cabinet members were devotees of Hamilton, who constantly worked to undermine him.

---

*And on one occasion had been a badly behaved pair. In 1786 they visited Shakespeare's home in Stratford-upon-Avon and chipped off a piece of the Bard's supposed chair as a souvenir.

How's this for a sharp put-down: 'Hamilton I know to be a proud spirited, conceited, aspiring mortal always pretending to morality, but with as debauched morals as old [Benjamin] Franklin who is more his model than anyone I know.'

Here are a few of the little difficulties Adams faced during his presidency:

The XYZ Affair
A strange name for a diplomatic tangle with the French. A delegation Adams sent to Paris in an attempt to improve frosty relations was kept waiting for days, allowed only fifteen minutes with the foreign minister Talleyrand and then found itself touched for eye-watering bribes before negotiations could begin. No deal!

The Quasi-War
Although Adams was keen to avoid the real thing, he had French ships harassed off the coast as a warning and persuaded Congress to finance the bolstering of the navy and the creation of an emergency army. This led to a peace treaty with France which had the effect of dividing his own party.

Alien and Sedition Acts

With passions aroused by the French Revolution fuelling a raging debate between individual freedoms and federal power in the US, Adams introduced a series of bills aimed (he argued) at preventing anarchy and ridding the country of French immigrants and other foreign nationals intent on stirring up insurrection against the state.

Not surprisingly these new powers were regarded by his opponents as repressive:

- The Naturalization Act made it harder for immigrants to become US citizens, raising the residency requirement from 5 to 14 years

- The Alien Enemies Act enabled the deportation of individuals who had arrived from a 'hostile nation'

- The Alien Friends Act allowed the president to imprison or deport non-citizens deemed dangerous

- The Sedition Act made it a criminal offence to make false statements critical of the federal government

free speech

If the wording of the Sedition Act seemed a potential threat to freedom of speech, Adams' Secretary of State, Timothy Pickering, made the threat real. He went on a witchhunt of the Jefferson Republicans.

John Fries's rebellion

In 1799, only a few years after the Whiskey Rebellion which Washington put down, Dutch farmers in Pennsylvania rose up against the tax Adams imposed to expand the navy in the Quasi-War with the French. Armed bands threatened the assessors in Quakertown and later liberated men who had been arrested for tax evasion. No blood was shed, and eventually the rebels were subdued by federal troops and the local militia.

The subsequent conviction of the ringleaders for treason was widely regarded as a gross overreaction. Adams later pardoned them all – including John Fries, an auctioneer who had first organised protest meetings and so gave the rebellion its name.

Pickering scoured newspapers for evidence of sedition against Adams and Congress. Editors and publishers were indicted and some papers closed down, while others were persuaded to tone down their criticism.

The most prominent case was the 1798 trial of Matthew Lyon, a Republican congressman from Vermont who had accused Adams of 'a continued grasp for power' and read out a letter at public meetings which asked why Congress hadn't sent the president to a madhouse.

- Sentenced to four months in jail and a $1,000 fine plus costs, he ran for re-election from his prison cell, and won

- His supporters petitioned Adams for a pardon, but the president refused it

- When he returned to Congress, the Federalists tried to expel him as a convicted criminal – and failed

You may guess who the winner was after this heavy clampdown on civil liberties – and it wasn't President John Adams.

'This is the most extraordinary collection of talent, of human knowledge, that has ever been gathered together at the White House, with the possible exception of when Thomas Jefferson dined alone.'

John F. Kennedy at a dinner honouring Nobel Prize winners

A Renaissance man

The election of 1800 was a close-run thing, but the Federalists were well beaten. For the first time both of the newly emerged parties fielded a joint ticket, with the Democratic-Republicans aiming to install Jefferson as president with Aaron Burr as his No. 2.

It happened eventually, but the two were initially tied on 73 electoral votes each, and it took all of 36 ballots in the House of Representatives to get there.

In **Thomas Jefferson** (1743–1826) the White House now had one of its most intellectual occupants – and the principal drafter, a quarter of a century earlier, of the stirring Declaration of Independence.

43

Mount Rushmore

It was devised as a tourist attraction for the Black Hills region of South Dakota,* but the carving of four presidents' faces in the granite eminence of Mount Rushmore is recognised as a national icon by millions around the world who couldn't point to its location on a map.

Created by the sculptor Gutzon Borglum and a team of 400 workers between 1927 and 1941, the work features George Washington, Thomas Jefferson, Theodore Roosevelt and Abraham Lincoln – four representatives of the first 130 years of the nation's history, he claimed, who preserved the republic and expanded its territory.

Each head is 18m (60ft) high. Their chief carver was Luigi del Bianco, an Italian immigrant renowned for his ability to etch emotions into stone.

Borglum got it right before he set to work: 'America will march along that skyline!'

The original idea was to celebrate heroes of the 'Wild West', such as Lewis and Clark, the Native American Red Cloud and Buffalo Bill.

He was a poor public speaker, which would have hampered his impact today, but apart from his political career he was something of a lawyer, a naturalist, an architect, an agronomist, a meteorologist,* an author, an inventor and a linguist.

Jefferson unfailingly appears in lists of the best presidents of all time – although critics aren't slow to point out significant ways in which he fell short of his own professed ideals.

- He pronounced that 'all men are created equal' but kept hundreds of slaves on his Monticello estate in Virginia, many of them harshly treated, and made no provision in his will, as Washington did, to free them

- He swiftly removed Adams' Sedition Act and pardoned those convicted under it, but later approved the use of libel laws against newspapers in Federalist Connecticut who persistently attacked him and his government

---

* He recorded the temperature in an ivory pocket book twice a day – rising at dawn for the first reading – and also tracked the patterns of winds and rainfall.

If that was hypocrisy, some other changes of direction can be put down to the pragmatism required by the job: he dismantled Hamilton's federalist fiscal system, for instance, but was persuaded by his treasury secretary to keep the national bank he had so roundly vilified.

Tackling the pirates

Jefferson also shrank the navy, but in 1801 he sent a fleet to the Mediterranean to make a stand against Barbary pirates who had long been capturing and pillaging US merchant ships and holding crew members for ransom.

Congress having rubber-stamped what was the new nation's first ever war, the American ships bombarded ports in present day Libya, Tunisia and Algeria. After the pasha of Tripoli captured the USS *Philadelphia*, Jefferson ordered a series of attacks on the city and forced a peace treaty on him.

Public opinion at home gave Jefferson the thumbs-up for this initiative – at once a victory for liberty over tyranny and a blow in favour of free trade.

A deal with Boney

Perhaps Jefferson's greatest achievement was practically doubling the size of his country in one bold stroke through **The Louisiana Purchase**, and then inspiring the colonisation of the 'Wild West'.

It was a case, though, of great good fortune – and of his reach far exceeding his intended grasp.

France owned a vast expanse of territory to the west of the United States, but Jefferson's prime concern was for the security of American shipping on the Mississippi down to the south. Would the French perhaps agree to sell some 100,000 sq km (40,000 square miles) in and around New Orleans?

In 1803 he sent two high-powered emissaries to Paris (the future president James Monroe and Robert R. Livingston, one of the five men who had signed the Declaration of Independence), with instructions to make an offer of around $10 million for the land.

He was about to get the shock of his life . . .

Word came back that Napoleon, strapped for the cash necessary to finance his wars, had made Monroe and Livingston a remarkable counter offer: he was prepared to sell all of 2,144,480 sq km (827,987 square miles) for $15 million.

The republican in Jefferson toyed with the idea that a constitutional amendment might be needed to sanction such a deal, but he sensed that there was no time to waste and his inner pragmatist once again came to the fore. The land was bought under the guise of a treaty – and it was sanctioned in October 1803 by a 24–7 vote in the Senate.

Lewis & Clark

Jefferson now turned his thoughts to the uncharted territory further west – and the need for the United States to colonise the area before the British and other Europeans did.

The expeditionary team he commissioned, with the backing of Congress, had the rather dull official title Corps of Discovery, but we know it best by the names of its two leaders.

Jefferson first chose the 29-year-old Meriwether Lewis, an outdoorsman and soldier (who had helped put down the Whiskey Rebellion), instructing him in navigation and mapping, natural history, mineralogy and astronomy, and giving him the free run of his extensive library at Monticello.

Lewis in turn co-opted his soldier friend William Clark, and they set off from St Louis in May 1804 with a band of US Army volunteers, charged with finding a watery Northwest Passage via the Mississippi from the Atlantic to the Pacific. (They failed.)

They returned two years and four months later, having mapped the land, made contact with more than seventy Native American tribes, collected numerous plant, seed and mineral specimens and filled their journals with the details of everything from Indian customs* to the geography, geology, climate and flora and fauna of the region.

---

* Clark, an unlettered man, is said to have spelt the word Sioux no fewer than 27 different ways in his journal.

A man of troubles

Vice presidents often operate under the radar, but Aaron Burr became accustomed to making the headlines – and for the wrong reasons.

As we've seen, in 1800 he was neck-and-neck with Jefferson in the race for the White House. He refused to stand aside even though the Democratic-Republican party had touted him as vice president. That caused bad blood between the two throughout Jefferson's first term.

The bad blood between Burr and Alexander Hamilton had more serious consequences. It may have first arisen when Burr won Hamilton's support for a much needed water company in Manhattan, only to change the charter and found a bank instead: people later died in a malaria epidemic, perhaps spread by contaminated water.

In 1804, knowing that he was about to be dropped by Jefferson, he ran for Governor of New York. During the campaign a letter published in the *Albany Register* claimed that Hamilton had called Burr 'a dangerous man, and one who ought not be trusted with the reins of government'.

After an exchange of letters between the two, Burr challenged Hamilton to a duel. They met at Weehawken, New Jersey, where Hamilton's son had been killed duelling three years before. Alas, like son, like father: Burr's shot pierced Hamilton's liver and spine, and he died the next day.

Although duelling was illegal, and although Burr was charged with multiple crimes, including murder, he was never tried. He briefly returned to his post as vice president, but after that his political career was over.

What he did next is open to interpretation, but it resulted in his standing trial for treason – with Jefferson pronouncing his guilt before the case had reached the courts.

Burr leased land in Louisiana; raised a band of armed men for 'hunting'; and was accused of planning to declare himself ruler of a new independent country in the region.

Chief Justice John Marshall acquitted Burr of treason in the face of Jefferson's energetic attempts to have him jailed – a defeat for the president and a victory for the principle of the Constitution's separation of powers between the executive and the judiciary.

Lewis and Clark have become legendary figures, but Jefferson launched several other, less spectacular expeditions – up the Ouachita River (1804–1805), along the Red River (1806) and into the Rocky Mountains and the south-west (1806–1807).

Closed for business

His second term was marred domestically by the Burr treason case and on the international stage by his response to British and French aggression on the high seas. He issued a proclamation banning armed British ships from US waters, while the Embargo Act of 1807 enforced a trade boycott with both countries.

It failed disastrously, throttling the US economy. Many merchants ignored the measure in desperation (and anger), and in effect became smugglers.

Jefferson revoked the embargo during the last days of his presidency – by which time he was so relieved to hand over the reins to his successor that he admitted feeling 'like a prisoner released from his chains'.

The War of 1812

Having served as Jefferson's Secretary of State, during which period he was responsible for supervising the Louisiana Purchase, **James Madison** (1751–1836) began two terms as president in 1809.

He's rightly honoured with the unofficial moniker Father of the Constitution, but his years in the top spot are, unhappily, best remembered for the burning of the White House.

It was the darn British again. During the war with Napoleon they were bolstering their crews with 'pressed' men, and many of these defected to US merchant vessels. In a tit-for-tat move American ships were seized and their sailors forced to join the navy – whether they were British subjects or not.

As the hostilities worsened Madison's ability to go to war was hampered by a divided cabinet and his own anti-federalist instincts: he had shrunk the army, lowered taxes and closed the national bank that he and Jefferson disliked.

We the people

James Madison made a major contribution to the US legal framework some thirty years before he became president. He was the prime mover behind the **Bill of Rights** – the first ten amendments to the Constitution.

During the bitter early protests by anti-federalists about the powers being given to Congress, Madison worked tirelessly to produce compromises which would allow governments sufficient clout in managing national affairs while acknowledging the separate rights of states and individuals.

Passed into law in 1789, the Bill of Rights gives specific guarantees of personal freedoms and imposes clear limitations on the government's power in judicial and other proceedings.

The tenth amendment in particular makes a ringing 'hands off!' declaration: 'The powers not delegated to the United States by the Constitution, nor prohibited by it to the States, are reserved to the States respectively, or to the people.'

At last, in June 1812, he asked Congress for a declaration of war – and when he got it could muster only a poorly trained militia.

Not surprisingly, the campaign got off to a bad start:

- Madison's initial plan was to capture Canada and use it as a bargaining tool, but the state militias in the north-east refused to take part

- The senior command was inept and / or cowardly, and at Detroit the US general surrendered to a smaller British force without firing a shot

- In the absence of the National Bank, Madison turned to New England financiers, and when they declined to help had to borrow at high interest rates from bankers in New York City and Philadelphia

At sea the US had more success. Madison authorised merchant vessels to become privateers (they captured as many as 1,800 British ships), and a naval shipyard with a workforce of thousands was established in New York, turning out a dozen warships.

The low point of the war from a morale point of view was the routing of the American troops at Bladensburg in Maryland in August 1814, followed by the capture and burning of Washington.

The White House and the Capitol were both set on fire – a heavy thunderstorm prevented their total destruction – and Madison took refuge in the small town of Brookeville, since proudly dubbed 'the United States Capital for a Day'.

Dolley to the rescue

Madison's wife Dolley, a great socialiser and the only First Lady to have been given an honorary seat on the floor of Congress, proved a heroine when the British set fire to the White House.

Before fleeing the building she insisted on rescuing an 8ft x 5ft portrait of George Washington rather than let it fall into enemy hands. It was fixed to the wall, so she had the frame broken, the canvas taken out 'and the precious portrait placed in the hands of two gentlemen from New York for safe keeping'.

The crucial American victory, effectively ending the war, was the Battle of New Orleans on January 8th, 1815, in which General Andrew Jackson inflicted heavy losses on the British – so securing the legendary status that would help propel him to the presidency fourteen years later.

feeling good

For a decade or more after the war, through the dying years of Madison's presidency and the following two terms under James Monroe, America seemed to take a deep breath and suppress its fierce party wranglings.

There's even a quaint name for this period of calm: The Era of Good Feelings.

It was impossible to imagine in this quietly maturing democracy that within forty years one of its greatest presidents would be witnessing the most terrible bloodletting ever suffered on American soil.

Army generals who became presidents

George Washington
Andrew Jackson
William Henry Harrison
Zachary Taylor
Franklin Pierce
Andrew Johnson
Ulysses S. Grant
Rutherford B. Hayes
James A. Garfield
Chester A. Arthur
Benjamin Harrison
Dwight D. Eisenhower

'Peace, above all things, is to be desired, but
blood must sometimes
be spilled to obtain it on equable
and lasting terms.'

Andrew Jackson

Not in my backyard

James Monroe (1758–1831) appears on some lists of the Founding Fathers, although he had no part in drafting the Declaration of Independence or the Constitution.

What he did create* was what has become known as the Monroe Doctrine – the warning to European nations that their interference in the affairs of any independent North or South American state would be regarded as 'the manifestation of an unfriendly disposition toward the United States'.

The other side of the coin was a promise that the US wouldn't interfere with internal matters of the European countries or with their existing colonies.

The doctrine has been interpreted in various ways over the years, with Latin Americans fearful that it lends itself to a controlling attitude towards them by the much more powerful United States.

---

* Although the text was written by his Secretary of State (and later President) John Quincy Adams.

'A house divided
against itself
cannot stand.'

CHAPTER TWO

IN TIME Of WAR

Every bit as craggy as his Mount Rushmore likeness, **Abraham Lincoln** (1809–1865) fought his presidential election campaign partly as a frontiersman from the sticks, born in a single-room log cabin in Kentucky; partly as Honest Abe, the gangly, plain-speaking fellow you could bet your bottom dollar on; and partly as a sophisticated lawyer with the gravitas of a potential national leader.

There was a truth to all these guises, but the man's essential qualities would emerge only through their testing in the fires of war and the struggle to save the Union from disintegration.

Trouble in Texas

Who owned Texas? Mexico, certainly, after winning its independence from Spain in 1821. The 'Texians' themselves, they said, when they revolted against the Mexican dictatorship in 1836 and established an independent republic inhabited mainly by US settlers. The United States, said President James K. Polk after annexing it as the 28th state of the Union in 1845.

The one-sided **Mexican-American War** of 1846–1848 left Mexico demoralised. Many Americans were cock-a-hoop over the further spread of their territory, but Abraham Lincoln was among the critics of the legality of the war and the way it was conducted.

The future president Ulysses S. Grant, then a young officer fighting for a cause he regarded as unjust, claimed in his memoirs that the conflict led to the Civil War itself.

'The Southern rebellion,' he wrote, 'was largely the outgrowth of the Mexican war. Nations, like individuals, are punished for their transgressions. We got our punishment in the most sanguinary and expensive war of modern times.'

He wasn't dirt poor, as the log cabin story suggests (his father owned and leased several farms in Kentucky before moving the family to Illinois), and he hated being called Abe (plain Lincoln suited him well), but the honesty and gravitas hit the mark.

Largely self-taught, he became a lawyer and was admitted to the Illinois bar in 1836.

- After representing a company against the owners of a riverboat that hit one of its bridges and sank, Lincoln invented a flotation device for boats in shallow water – and he's the only president to hold a patent (no. 6469 1849), although it was never taken up

- In his most successful criminal case he challenged a witness who claimed to have seen a murder in the moonlight by producing a Farmers' Almanac to show that the position of the Moon that night seriously reduced visibility

- In 1859 he persuaded the judge to reverse a decision to exclude evidence favourable to a woman charged with stabbing her cousin to death – and she was eventually acquitted

The Great Debates

All this time Lincoln was building up a head of steam in his political career. In 1858, as a Republican pitching for an Illinois seat in the Senate, he took on the local Democrat, Stephen A. Douglas, in a series of seven 'Great Debates' that drew crowds of thousands.

Slavery was the major theme. Douglas had drafted the Kansas-Nebraska Act of 1854, which not only opened up those states to thousands of settlers but gave them the right to decide whether slavery should exist in the territory.

Lincoln accused the Act of having a '*declared* indifference, but as I must think, a covert *real zeal* for the spread of slavery'.

And in a famous speech in the Illinois State Capitol he said, 'A house divided against itself cannot stand. I believe this government cannot endure, permanently, half slave and half free. I do not expect the Union to be dissolved — I do not expect the house to fall — but I do expect it will cease to be divided.'

Lincoln narrowly lost that Senate race, but he now had a formidable national reputation and was being touted for the presidency. In February 1860, unsure of his popularity in the north-east of the country, he seized the chance of giving a speech to a powerful group of Republicans in New York.

'No man,' reported the journalist Noah Brooks, 'ever before made such an impression on his first appeal to a New York audience.'

He was on his way!

No holds barred

Several presidents were keen wrestlers in their youth and have been honoured in the National Wrestling Hall of Fame, but none of them has attracted the mythology surrounding Lincoln.

According to the most bullish stories he fought no fewer than 300 bouts and lost only once. Asked about this while on the campaign trail, he's said to have admitted being 'dusted' by someone called Lorenzo Dow Thompson.

'I am in height six feet, four inches, nearly; lean in flesh, weighing, on an average, one hundred and eighty pounds; dark complexion, with coarse black hair and gray eyes – no other marks or brands recollected.'

Lincoln's note for his 1860 campaign PR team

His promoters called him The Rail Candidate, evoking the days when he had cleared the land with his father and (reluctantly, since he would rather read a book) split fence rails with an axe.

And in the Wide Awakes they energised young people in a mass movement that wouldn't be out of place in a modern political campaign.*

They organised popular social events, produced comic books and marched through cities in the north-east and the border states in a uniform of capes and glazed black hats while carrying large burning torches. Their standard banner was a large eyeball.

---

* It would later become a paramilitary organisation, and so disturbed politicians in the southern states that they formed their own militias, the Minutemen.

Secession

At Chicago in May 1860 Lincoln won the Republican nomination on the third ballot. Six months later, in a four-way tussle, he emerged victorious as the 16th president of the United States – and the turmoil began.

South Carolina moved first, seceding from the Union in December – so jumping the gun of Lincoln's presidency by more than ten weeks. Florida, Mississippi, Alabama, Georgia, Louisiana and Texas quickly followed suit, the breakaway states declaring themselves a sovereign nation (the Confederate States of America), with Jefferson Davies as their provisional president.

Lincoln, arriving in Washington in disguise (*page 83*), made it clear in his inauguration address in March that although he hated slavery and wanted it outlawed in the newly colonised territories, 'I have no purpose, directly or indirectly, to interfere with the institution of slavery in the states where it exists. I believe I have no lawful right to do so, and I have no inclination to do so.'

He ended with an eloquent message to the South, claiming that the two sides were friends, rather than enemies.

> The mystic chords of memory, stretching from every battlefield and patriot grave to every living heart and hearthstone all over this broad land, will yet swell the chorus of the Union when again touched, as surely they will be, by the better angels of our nature.

But it was too late for fine words or a debate about the states' constitutional rights. Although Lincoln was slow to realise it, the South already regarded itself at war.

Birth of a party

Lincoln was the first Republican president. The Grand Old Party (or GOP) as it's often known today, was established in 1854 by a coming together of anti-slavery activists, Whigs (Lincoln had been one) and former National Republicans.

The Democrats trace their beginnings to the Democratic-Republican Party founded by Jefferson and Hamilton in 1828.

On April 12, 1861, Confederate forces launched a sustained bombardment of Fort Sumter in the harbour at Charleston, South Carolina, forcing its garrison to surrender. Lincoln responded by calling on the states to provide 75,000 troops 'to preserve the Union', although he fondly imagined that they would be needed for only ninety days.

Obliged to decide which side it was on, Virginia immediately joined the rebel states, with Arkansas, Tennessee and North Carolina following close behind.

Civil War

In the bitter American Civil War, fought from 1861 to 1865, the dead were estimated to have numbered at least 620,000 – more than the US has lost in all its other wars combined.

As commander-in-chief, Lincoln controlled the overall strategy of the conflict, but – no soldier himself – he entrusted tactical matters to his generals in the field. The greatest of these was the man he eventually promoted to the heady title of lieutenant general, Ulysses S. Grant.

The two men had similar personalities. John Eaton, an army chaplain put in charge of caring for black slaves passing through Union lines, met them both.

'In my association with Lincoln and with Grant, I think what impressed me most was the fact that their greatness rested in both cases upon the simple and fundamental elements of character.

'Both were essentially sane in morals and intellect. Both were normal men first and great men afterwards.'

The power of speech

Both, too, were implacable in their drive to save the Union, but only Lincoln had that magical mastery of the language that could sway minds to a cause.

On January 1st, 1863, he refined that cause in his Emancipation Proclamation: it was not only to preserve the precious Union but to give freedom to all the slaves (approaching four million of them) in the rebellious states.

'He fights!'

Ulysses S. Grant (1822–1885) graduated from West Point in 1843 and served with distinction in the Mexican-American War, but resigned soon afterwards, acknowledging that the boredom of non-combative life had literally driven him to drink.

He spent seven troubled years in civvy street, at one time selling firewood from street corners, before the Civil War drew him back. He quickly rose to the rank of general, and was given overall command of the Union Army in March 1864. Earlier in the campaign other military men had criticised his tactics, but Lincoln is said to have replied: 'I can't spare this man – he fights!'

After the death of Lincoln and the impeachment of his successor, Andrew Johnson, Grant accepted nomination for the presidency with reluctance, feeling that only he could unite a divided nation. His two terms were marked, on the negative side, by corruption within the administration, on the positive side by a series of reforms which forced Reconstruction on the southern states and improved the lot of African Americans and American Indians.

In November of that year, months after the bloody battle of Gettysburg which had turned the war in the Union's favour, he arrived at the site for the consecration of a national cemetery.

The Gettysburg Address* wasn't billed as a major speech – someone else gave a two-hour 'Oration' while the president was called on only to make 'Dedicatory remarks' – but it has reverberated through the ages.

Four score and seven years ago our fathers brought forth on this continent, a new nation, conceived in Liberty, and dedicated to the proposition that all men are created equal.

Now we are engaged in a great civil war, testing whether that nation, or any nation so conceived and so dedicated, can long endure. We are met on a great battlefield of that war. We have come to dedicate a portion of that field, as a final resting place for those who here gave their lives that that nation might live. It is altogether fitting and proper that we should do this.

---

* *Five different versions have survived. This is the one that appears on the Lincoln Memorial in Washington.*

But, in a larger sense, we cannot dedicate –
we cannot consecrate – we cannot hallow –
this ground. The brave men, living and dead,
who struggled here, have consecrated it, far
above our poor power to add or detract.

The world will little note, nor long remember
what we say here, but it can never forget what
they did here. It is for us the living, rather,
to be dedicated here to the unfinished work
which they who fought here have thus far so
nobly advanced.

It is rather for us to be here dedicated to
the great task remaining before us – that
from these honored dead we take increased
devotion to that cause for which they gave the
last full measure of devotion – that we here
highly resolve that these dead shall not have
died in vain that this nation, under God,
shall have a new birth of freedom – and that
government of the people, by the people, for
the people, shall not perish from the earth.

The silver tongue wagged above an iron
resolve. Lincoln commanded the destruction of
the South's railroads, bridges and plantations
in order to bring the rebels to heel.

They also served

They ranked well below Ulysses S. Grant, but four other future presidents fought for the Union during the Civil War.

Rutherford Hayes (1822–1893) initially had a 'let them go' attitude to the southern states, but he left his law practice in his late thirties to join the army, was injured several times and was promoted to the honorary rank of brevet major general for his bravery.

A teacher turned career politician, **James Garfield** (1831–1881) volunteered at the age of 29, took command of a brigade and ended the war as a major general.

Another lawyer, **Benjamin Harrison** (1833–1901) commanded a brigade and at the end of the war was awarded the grade of brevet brigadier general of volunteers.

William McKinley (1843–1901) enlisted at the age of 18, was promoted to second lieutenant for his bravery in battle and later survived having a horse shot under him. He ended as a brevet major. He would become the last US 19th century war leader, president during the **Spanish–American War** of 1898.

By the end of 1864 the Confederacy was eager to talk peace terms, but Lincoln refused to allow any negotiations which appeared to put the two sides on an equal footing.

On the stump again

All through the later stages of the war Lincoln had his mind on the next election – and the real possibility that he might lose it. He worked tirelessly to bring together not only opposing factions within his own party, but supportive Democrats, too.

When campaigning began, the Republicans actually adopted a temporary change of name to the Union Party and chose a 'War Democrat', Andrew Johnson, as vice president on their ticket.

Lincoln was so doubtful of winning that he signed a secret pledge that, should the worst happen, 'it will be my duty to so co-operate with the President elect, as to save the Union between the election and the inauguration'.

He won by a landslide.

Presidents at war

American Revolution 1775-1783
  George Washington

War of 1812
  James Madison

Mexican-American War 1846-1848
  James K. Polk

US Civil War 1861-1865
  Abraham Lincoln

Spanish American War 1898
  William McKinley

World War I 1914-1918
  Woodrow Wilson

World War II 1939-1945
  Franklin D. Roosevelt and Harry S. Truman

Korean War 1950-1953
  Dwight D. Eisenhower

Vietnam War 1960-1975
  Dwight D. Eisenhower, John F. Kennedy,
  Lyndon B. Johnson, and Richard Nixon

Persian Gulf War 1990-1991
  George H. W. Bush

Second Persian Gulf War 2003-2010
  George W. Bush and Barack Obama

Lincoln's greatness lies in part in the generous terms he promoted for the South once the war had been won. 'Let 'em up easy,' was how he put it to one Union general.

In his second inauguration speech, two months before the Confederate forces surrendered at Appomattox in May, 1865, he looked forward to a time of healing.

Those wounds would take many years to heal, but he wouldn't be there to see the work through.

"Honey, I forgot to duck"

CHAPTER THREE

THE ASSASSIN'S BULLET

On the night of April 14th, 1865, the celebrated actor and ardent Confederate sympathiser John Wilkes Booth stepped into a box at Ford's Theatre in Washington, cocked his Derringer pistol and, after waiting for a burst of laughter from the audience to cover the sound, shot Abraham Lincoln in the back of the head. He died at 7.22 the following morning.

With four incumbents shot dead, two more injured in assassination attempts and several others having had close escapes, taking on the US presidency is an act of courage.

Before their time 1

Apart from those who were assassinated, four presidents have died in office.

William Henry Harrison (1773–1841) chose to play the role of macho man for his oath of office on a cold and wet March day. He rode on horseback rather than in a carriage and declined to wear a hat or overcoat. But was that really why, as is widely suggested, he died of pneumonia only 31 days into his term? The fact is that he didn't fall ill until three weeks later, when doctors tried various cures, including opium, castor oil, leeches and Virginia snakeweed. Modern thinking is that he died of enteric fever because the White House lay downstream of open sewers.

Zachary Taylor (1784–1850) fell ill during a fund-raising event at the Washington Memorial on Independence Day and died in the White House five days later. The diagnosis was gastroenteritis, perhaps caused by the large quantities of iced milk, cold cherries and pickles he'd enjoyed. Some suspected that he had been poisoned by anti-slavery southerners, but it's more likely that those wretched sewers had struck twice within a decade.

Booth's attack followed an earlier, failed attempt to abduct Lincoln and hold him to ransom, and was part of a conspiracy which would on the same night have eliminated Vice President Andrew Johnson (his would-be assailant lost his nerve) and Secretary of State William H. Seward (who was stabbed by David Herold, but later recovered).

Ulysses S. Grant had also been singled out. He was supposed to have been at the play with Lincoln, but their two wives didn't get on and he made his excuses.

The ensuing manhunt was the most intensive in US history, with large rewards on offer and thousands of federal troops and countless civilians on the look-out. When Booth and Herold were surprised sleeping in a barn by the 16th New York Cavalry twelve days later, the wild actor decided on a dramatic last act. Wielding a pistol and a rifle, he escaped through a back door and was shot – fittingly, in the back of the head.

Four of the conspirators were hanged, Mary Surratt being the first woman ever executed by the US Government.

Lilacs

Lincoln's death was lamented in the South as well as the North – and also abroad, where many countries issued proclamations and declared periods of mourning.

He was, Ulysses S. Grant said, 'incontestably the greatest man I ever knew.'

Walt Whitman wrote elegies to the lost leader, including 'Oh Captain! My Captain!' and 'When Lilacs Last in the Dooryard Bloom'd', which begins:

When lilacs last in the dooryard bloom'd,
And the great star early droop'd in the western
  sky in the night,
I mourn'd … and yet shall mourn with
  ever-returning spring.

O ever-returning spring! trinity sure to me
  you bring;
Lilac blooming perennial, and drooping star in
  the west
And thought of him I love.

Special trains brought thousands to the capital, some sleeping on the Capitol lawn, and mourners lined up seven abreast for a full mile to view Lincoln in his walnut casket in the black-draped East Room of the White House.

On April 19th there were vast crowds to watch the funeral procession, while millions later lined the 2,700km (1,700-mile) route of the train taking his remains from New York to Springfield, Illinois.

The Baltimore Plot

Some ten years after founding the detective agency that still bears his name, Allan Pinkerton persuaded Lincoln that he had uncovered a plot to kill him in Baltimore on the way to his inauguration in Washington.

He disguised the president in a long cape and a Tam o'Shanter, and his train secretly passed through the town at night. Many thought the plot a fabrication, and the press later lampooned Lincoln, painting him as a coward. Did they perhaps remember their disdain four years later?

Before their time 2

Warren Harding (1865–1923) died in mysterious circumstances. On the way back from the first ever presidential visit to Alaska he developed what seemed to be a bad case of food poisoning. Arriving in San Francisco, he took to his bed at the Palace Hotel with pneumonia, dying soon afterwards either of a stroke (New York Times) or a heart attack (naval doctors). He had many political enemies and was routinely unfaithful to his wife, so when she refused permission for an autopsy to be carried out, suspicions were aroused.

Franklin D. Roosevelt (1882–1945) was unable to walk unaided after contracting a paralytic illness in his early thirties, but he disguised his handicap in public appearances by wearing leg braces and being supported by an aide. His death, not connected to this condition, followed a period of declining health perhaps made worse by the rigours of leading his country through the Second World War. Resting at his personal retreat in Georgia before the founding conference of the United Nations, he complained of 'a terrific headache' and died of a cerebral haemorrhage.

Dodgy doctors

The only sitting member of the House of Representatives to be elected president, **James A. Garfield** was just four months into the job when, in July 1881, he was shot at the Baltimore and Potomac railroad station by an unhinged Republican who thought Vice President Chester A. Arthur should be running the country. (He got his wish.)

Charles Guiteau was a penniless failed lawyer, would-be theologian and political crank who had once lobbied the party in favour of Garfield's candidacy. He seemed to think this entitled him to a government job, and the one he chose was the US consulship in Paris – although he spoke not a word of French.

When this absurd ambition was refused he took the side of the anti-Garfield 'Stalwart' faction in the party – we'll spare you details of the rift – and bought himself an ivory handled revolver which, he said later, would look good when displayed in a museum in the years to come. (He didn't get his wish, because the weapon later went missing.)

Despite plausible claims that he was insane,* Guiteau was hanged for the murder the following July.

But was he completely to blame? He argued in his defence that although he had fired the shot, it was Garfield's doctors who had done for him, and he probably had a point – with today's medical knowledge he would probably have been back on his feet within days.

Guiteau had fired two shots, with one bullet glancing off Garfield's arm and the other lodging in his stomach. Alexander Graham Bell, who had recently invented the telephone, unsuccessfully tried to find the slug with a primitive metal detector, while the medical team probed his wound with bare and unsterilised hands.

Eleven weeks after he was shot, the weakened president died from a massive infection.

---

* During his trial he cursed the judge, recited his testimony via epic poems and canvassed spectators in the court for legal advice. He later dictated his life story to the New York Herald, appending a personal ad for 'a nice Christian lady under 30 years of age'.

Near misses 1

Apart from those presidents who took a bullet, several others survived attempts on their lives.

In January 1835 Richard Lawrence, a house painter, tried to shoot **Andrew Jackson**, but both his pistols misfired. He was later confined to a mental institution.

During the first summit between the US and Mexico, in October 1909, an armed would-be assassin was arrested only feet away from **William Taft** and his Mexican counterpart, Porfirio Diaz.

Herbert Hoover was targeted by anarchists while on a goodwill tour of Central and South America in 1928. They planned to blow up his train as it crossed Argentina, but the bomber was arrested before he could place the explosives on the rails.

Alerted by British intelligence, the US Secret Service in 1947 intercepted and defused letter bombs sent by the Zionist Stern Gang and intended for **Harry S. Truman** and members of his White House staff.

A security lapse

A visit to the Pan-American Exposition at the Temple of Music in Buffalo, New York, perhaps seemed a run-of-the-mill engagement for **William McKinley** to make on that September day in 1901, but his personal secretary, George Courtelyou, was so worried about the potential danger involved that he had twice taken it off the presidential schedule.

McKinley, who enjoyed meeting people and regularly pushed away protection by security officers, twice restored it – and he was happily mingling with an appreciative public when a man whose right hand seemed to be wrapped in a handkerchief let it slip to reveal a revolver. He fired twice.

This was Leon Czolgosz, the son of Polish immigrants, who had turned to anarchism after losing his job in the economic depression known as 'The Panic of 1893'. As he prepared to pull the trigger for a third time, he was overpowered, thrown to the ground and furiously battered, until the stricken president called for the violence to stop.

There are echoes in McKinley's decline and death of the fate that befell Garfield twenty years earlier – although his demise was much swifter. Like Garfield, he was hit in the stomach, at first seemed to be making a recovery, but then took a turn for the worse.

There was no metal detector from Alexander Graham Bell this time, but another notable inventor, Thomas Edison, sent an X-ray machine from New Jersey. In the event it wasn't used and, again, there are questions to be answered about the precautions doctors took against infections.

Gangrene, his biographer wrote, 'was creeping along the bullet's track through the stomach, the pancreas, and one kidney'. He died twelve days after being shot, having acknowledged that the end was inevitable: 'It is useless, gentlemen,' he is reported to have said. 'I think we ought to have prayer.'

After Czolgosz was sentenced to death in the electric chair, Congress passed legislation designating the Secret Service as the agency in charge of presidential security.

Near misses 2

Three years after the letter bomb scare, in 1950, two Puerto Rican pro-independence activists attempted to kill **Harry S. Truman**. One of them was shot dead by a White House policeman, who later died of his wounds, while the other was seriously injured.

In 1974 Samuel Byck tried to hijack a commercial airliner with the intention of crashing it into the White House and killing **Richard Nixon**. After a gunfight he committed suicide.

Only two women have tried to assassinate a US president – both of them targeting **Gerald Ford** in September 1975. On the first occasion the gun failed to fire; on the second a bystander intervened and the shot missed.

Truck driver Frank Corder flew a small Cessna on to the White House lawn in 1994, apparently hoping to smash into the building and kill **Bill Clinton**: in fact he hit a tree and was himself killed. There were further attempts on the life of Clinton and his wife Hillary over the years – via semi-automatic rifle fire, a car bomb, a pipe bomb and a letter bomb.

Death in Dallas

Shortly after midday on November 22nd, 1963, as his presidential motorcade drove through waving crowds in downtown Dallas, shots from a high-powered rifle rang out and John F. Kennedy slumped in his seat, fragments of his brain spattering the car's interior.

With him in the Lincoln Continental four-door convertible were the governor of Texas, John Connally (who was seriously injured, but survived), and their two wives.

This much is indisputable – but, despite two subsequent exhaustive investigations, controversy still rages about how many shots were fired and whether Lee Harvey Oswald, the man arrested for the killing, acted alone.

To this day, a majority of Americans believe that there was a cover-up, with conspiracy theories pointing an accusing finger at groups and individuals as varied as the Mafia, the CIA, the Russian KGB, Cuban leader Fidel Castro and even Kennedy's vice president, Lyndon B. Johnson.

The Second Amendment

Why on earth, ask so many non-Americans, doesn't the country do something about its 'gun culture'? After all, with around 90 weapons for every 100 residents, and their presence in some 40 per cent of homes, the US has by far the highest murder rate in the developed world.

The short answer is the Second Amendment: 'A well regulated Militia being necessary to the security of a free State, the right of the people to keep and bear Arms shall not be infringed.'

Never mind that the Bill of Rights (page 54) was created for a very different age, it's a brave government that dares to stand between citizens and their guns – although high profile killings have led to some tinkering with the law in modern times.

The Kennedy assassination, and the murders soon afterwards of his brother (and likely future president) Robert and the activists Malcolm X and Martin Luther King, led to the Gun Control Act of 1968. This outlawed the selling of firearms to individuals deemed to be 'prohibited persons'.

> 'I have a very strict gun control policy: if there's a gun around,
> I want to be in control of it.'
>
> *Clint Eastwood, actor*

After the attempt on Ronald Reagan's life, the 1993 'Brady Law' established a national background check system to prevent weapons getting into the wrong hands.

The following year Bill Clinton signed a bill into law prohibiting the manufacture of assault weapons for civilian use. It expired after ten years, and although Barack Obama said he wanted to reinstate it – 'weapons that were designed for soldiers in war theatres don't belong on our streets' – he got nowhere with Congress.

After a series of school massacres which led to hundreds of thousands marching in favour of tighter controls, Donald Trump suggested that arming teachers was the solution. In 2018 he gave a speech in favour of gun rights to the powerful National Rifle Association ahead of the midterm elections, its vice chairman, Wayne La Pierre, asserting that the only march that mattered was 'the march to the polls on election day'.

Near misses 3

While **George W. Bush** was giving a speech in Tbilisi in 2005 a Georgian national, Vladimir Arutyunian, threw a live hand grenade towards the podium. It failed to explode – and Bush knew nothing of the attempt until later.

In 2009 security services uncovered a plot by four men with knives to assassinate **Barack Obama** at the Alliance of Civilizations summit in Istanbul. Two years later an unemployed 21-year-old sprayed the White House with semi-automatic fire (the family was away); in 2013 Obama was sent a letter laced with the deadly poison ricin; while in 2018 a package containing a pipe bomb was sent to his home in Washington and intercepted by the Secret Service.

In 2016 a disturbed 20-year-old British man attempted to grab a policeman's gun in order to shoot **Donald Trump**. A year later an Islamic State plot to assassinate him during the ASEAN summit was foiled by the Philippine National Police, while in 2018 the Secret Service intercepted a letter containing ricin sent to him by a US Navy veteran, William Clyde Allen III.

Few doubt the involvement of Oswald, a former US Marine, and a communist who had spent some time in Russia. He worked at the Texas School Book Depository from which at least some of the shots had been fired, his Italian Carcano rifle was found in a sixth-floor room and within an hour of the assassination, on the run, he had shot dead a police officer with a pistol. He was soon arrested.

But did he have accomplices? Here's where more than a hundred 'ear witnesses' thought the shots had come from:

The book depository 51.9%
A 'grassy knoll' overlooking the route 31.7%
Two separate locations 4.8%
Either depository or grassy knoll 2.9%
Somewhere else entirely 8.7%

Enter Jack Ruby

During his interrogation at Dallas police headquarters, Oswald claimed that he had been framed, but thanks to the brutal intervention of a shady nightclub owner, Jack Ruby, this defence would never be tested.

Two days after the assassination, as Oswald was being led through the basement of the police building on his way to the nearby county jail, Ruby stepped from a crowd of reporters and fired a single round from a revolver into his stomach. He died soon afterwards.

Ruby said he had been enraged by Kennedy's killing, but as he had a network of criminal connections, suspicious minds felt that someone had paid him to stop Oswald talking.

Detective work

The **Warren Commission**, set up to investigate the assassination, delivered an 888-page report with twenty-six volumes of supporting documents, including the testimony of more than 550 witnesses. It found that:

- Three shots had been fired, all by Lee Harvey Oswald
- Oswald had acted alone
- Two of the bullets struck Kennedy from behind
- One of the bullets passed through Kennedy's body before hitting Governor Connally

Remarkably, four of the seven men on the commission had doubts about the report's conclusions – and likewise the public at large.

Only the idea of a 'magic bullet' (Exhibit CE 399) that hit both men could justify the conclusion that Oswald had acted alone. If Kennedy and Connally were hit by separate bullets, the timing showed that they couldn't have been fired from the one bolt-action rifle. Had there been *four* bullets, with a second assailant on that grassy knoll?

In a response to the widespread scepticism, the **United States House Select Committee on Assassinations** was set up twelve years later, charged with examining the deaths both of President Kennedy and Martin Luther King.

Although it criticised Warren and government agencies for performing with 'varying degrees of efficiency' in compiling the earlier report, its findings were broadly similiar until, late in the day, it heard acoustic recordings suggesting that four bullets had, indeed, been fired.

Verdict: there had been a conspiracy.

Down but not out

Two presidents took a bullet from would-be assassins, but survived – with a smile!

In October 1912 **Theodore Roosevelt** was campaigning for the presidency in Milwaukee when he was shot by a deranged saloon keeper, John Schrank. By a huge stroke of luck the bullet was slowed by passing through a thick notebook in his jacket before lodging in his chest. He refused to go to hospital until he had finished his speech. 'I have just been shot,' he told his audience, 'but it takes more than that to kill a Bull Moose.'

Ronald Reagan was only two months into his presidency in March 1981 when, as he left the Washington Hilton hotel, a bullet fired by John Hinckley Jr lodged in his left lung less than 25mm (an inch) from his heart. The notoriously laid-back Reagan was still conscious in hospital when his wife Nancy visited, telling her 'Honey, I forgot to duck'. Before being taken off to the operating theatre he scribbled a note to a nurse, echoing the famous would-be epitaph of the actor and comedian W.C. Fields: 'All in all, I'd rather be in Philadelphia.'

Alas, the interpretation of these recordings was later found to be erroneous – throwing the whole debate wide open once again.

Years later the Committee's chief counsel, Robert Blakey, regretted that the role of the CIA hadn't been properly investigated: 'We now know that the Agency withheld from the Warren Commission the CIA-Mafia plots to kill Castro. Had the commission known of the plots, it would have followed a different path in its investigation.'

Cometh the hour

In the shocked aftermath of the assassination, with Kennedy mourned around the world, Lyndon B. Johnson (aka LBJ) stepped up to the presidency.

He had a reputation as a domineering, foul-mouthed Texan with a talent for bending other politicians to his will. This he now did in the interests of social security, wilderness preservation and, above all, civil rights . . .

'We have come to a
time of testing. We
must not fail.'

CHAPTER FOUR

BLACK AND WHITE

When Barack Obama, a former lawyer, civil rights attorney and professor, became president in January 2009, the US seemed to be signalling an end to centuries of wretched interracial strife. He was its very first African American commander-in-chief.

He was followed into the White House by a man who questioned Obama's birthright and campaigned on a platform that demonised immigrants – reminding the world that the healing of those grievous wounds was still unfinished business after all.

Slave culture

The early US economy was so dependent upon forced slave labour that among the first twelve presidents only John Adams and his son John Quincy never owned any.

That's not to say that the rest of them shared a common attitude to what we now regard as an abomination. George Washington, as we've seen, at least freed his in his will, while James Monroe, although he kept 75, is honoured for promoting the resettling of freed slaves in Africa.*

Some of the others have a shabbier record.

- **Thomas Jefferson kept more than 600 slaves at Monticello. After his wife's death he is believed to have fathered several children with her half-sister thirty years his junior, the enslaved Sally Hemings. A DNA analysis in 1998 gave this theory strong backing.**

---

* *Only two national capitals are named after American presidents: Washington in the USA and Monrovia in Liberia.*

- William Henry Harrison at one time declared himself an abolitionist – but when he became the first governor of the Indiana territory he tried to legalise slavery, and he later condemned the idea of equal rights for emancipated slaves.

- Although James Polk later freed slaves in his will, he defeated Martin Van Buren, his chief rival for the Democratic presidential nomination, by declaring his toleration of slavery.

Native Americans too

No former national hero has had his reputation as tarnished by his treatment of minorities as Andrew Jackson, the great war leader and promoter of the westward expansion many Americans saw as their 'manifest destiny'.

As a slave owner and trader, he was a vicious 'master', beating and whipping those who stepped out of line, let alone dared to escape. And then, once president, he introduced the Indian Removal Act of 1830 which drove some 50,000 Native Americans from their lands.

Many died as they trekked thousands of miles, some bound in chains, along what became known as the Trail of Tears to designated 'Indian territory' across the Mississipi river in present day Oklahoma.

Jackson, who had long advocated 'Indian removal' and had, as an army general, driven out the Creek and Seminole tribes to free land for white farmers, claimed that they had 'neither the intelligence, the industry, the moral habits, nor the desire of improvement which are essential to any favorable change in their condition'.

They must, he said chillingly, 'necessarily yield to the force of circumstances and ere long disappear'.

Federal law stipulated that dispersal should be arranged through treaties, and these were rigorously applied. In 1838, after a few self-appointed representatives of the Cherokee Nation accepted $5 million for their land in Georgia, the many who resented the agreement and stayed put were cruelly displaced by Van Buren's government.

An army 7,000 strong was sent to force the Cherokee into stockades at bayonet point, while their homes were freely looted, and then to march them 12,000 miles into Indian territory.

It's estimated that more than 5,000 died – from exhaustion and from the effects of diseases such as whooping cough, cholera, typhus and dysentery.

A guilty secret

What the early settlers liked to call the 'Five Civilised Tribes' – the Cherokee, Chickasaw, Choctaw, Creek and Seminole nations – were those who (before the Indian removal began) best accommodated themselves to the European incomers.

But if they shared some of the colonial virtues (literacy, commerce, written constitutions, centralised governments), they also shared a glaring vice: slavery. Even before the arrival of Europeans, they would make slaves of captured Native Americans from other tribes. Later they would enslave and trade black Africans too.

After Lincoln

Choosing the Democrat Andrew Johnson (1767–1845) as his running mate had been a smart unifying move by Abraham Lincoln during the Civil War (*page 75*), but it proved calamitous after his assassination.

On Johnson's watch, and to his chagrin, several Reconstruction laws addressed the injustices suffered by African Americans:

- In December 1865 the 13th Amendment to the Constitution abolished slavery

- The following year the Civil Rights Act made everyone born in the US a citizen, regardless of race, colour or 'previous condition'

- The 14th amendment of 1868 ruled that all persons born or naturalised in the USA were American citizens – except for Indians on reservations

- The 15th amendment of 1870 prohibited the federal government and individual states from denying a citizen the right to vote based on 'race, colour or previous condition of servitude'

Johnson, though in favour of upholding the Union, was an unrepentant sympathiser of the Southern cause who, as president, obstructed reform as doggedly as he could.

When the Civil Rights Bill landed on his desk he vetoed it, claiming that it discriminated in favour of African Americans over whites. Congress promptly overrode the veto – the first time in the nation's history that this had ever happened with a major bill.

Most of the southern states were still outside the Union, awaiting their submission to the new legislation. Johnson fought as hard as he could to get them a special deal, allowing them to grant only limited suffrage to former slaves, but he was now locked in a bitter battle with Congress he couldn't win.

By 1870, with Ulysses S. Grant now in the White House, all the rebel states had come back into the fold. They were, of course, legally bound by the same rules as the rest of the country – but the desperation and anger of the defeated South gave its black inhabitants only a pyrrhic victory.

A fifth of its young men of conscription age had been killed in the Civil War. Towns had been burned down, farms lay in waste and its road, rail and riverboat infrastructure had been destroyed.

Slavery had gone, but state and local 'Jim Crow' laws (taking their name from an abusive word for blacks) soon forced a blatant racial segregation which left African Americans as second-class citizens. Further leglislation even contrived to eat away at their voting rights.

A second Reconstruction was sorely needed – but it wouldn't arrive for the best part of a hundred years.

Bending the Constitution

The phrase used to justify racial segregation in the southern states was 'separate but equal' – referring to the 14th Amendment which guaranteed all people 'equal protection'. This interpretation was confirmed by the Supreme Court in 1896, although the supposed equality was a cruel charade: most African Americans were second-class citizens with substantially poorer health, education and income.

Rights and wrongs

Assessing the best and worst human rights records of American leaders from 1900 to the Obama presidency might seem an impossible task, but in 2017 the *Washington Post* reported the meticulous research of a political science professor at Northwestern University.

What Alvin B. Tillery had done was examine the 'positive tone' regarding civil rights and race relations in the editorials of no fewer than 9,406 African American writers in 43 black-controlled newspapers over that long period. This produced a (perhaps surprising) best-to-worst 'editorial opinion score'.

1 Lyndon B. Johnson
2 Dwight D. Eisenhower
3 Franklin D. Roosevelt
4 Harry Truman
5 Warren Harding
6 Theodore Roosevelt
7 Barack Obama
8 John F. Kennedy
9 Gerald Ford
10 Bill Clinton
11 Calvin Coolidge
12 William Taft
13 Jimmy Carter
14 Richard Nixon
15 Ronald Reagan
16 Woodrow Wilson
17 George H.W. Bush
18 George W. Bush
19 Herbert Hoover

Whatever their achievements in other areas, it's easy to understand why Woodrow Wilson and Herbert Hoover feature in the basement area of Tillery's statistical civil rights edifice.

Wilson (1856–1924) led the country through the First World War and has been praised for championing the new League of Nations at the Paris Peace Conference of 1919 (although he failed to persuade Senate that the US should join it). Domestically, though, he displayed the instincts of a typical southern Democrat.

- When, as a political scientist, he became president of Princeton University in 1902, he discouraged blacks from applying for admission

- Although he drafted African American soldiers into the army and gave them equal pay, he kept them in all-black units under white officers

- He enforced separate workspaces, lunchrooms and lavatories in government offices, while at the Post Office Department he downgraded many African Americans and put them behind screens in order to keep them out of public view

'The white men of the South were aroused by the mere instinct of self-preservation to rid themselves, by fair means or foul, of the intolerable burden of governments sustained by the votes of ignorant negroes.'

Woodrow Wilson: A History of the American People

- In his various writings (see above) he praised the 'great' Ku Klux Klan,* notorious for its lynchings of blacks, as 'a veritable empire of the South, to protect the Southern country'.

Lily-whites

Herbert Hoover (1874–1924), a lifelong Quaker famous for his humanitarian food relief work during the First World War, fought the 1928 election on a shamelessly racist platform – supporting the 'Lily-white' faction within the Republican party in an attempt to win over southern whites who, since the Civil War, had voted Democrat. He won by a landslide.

---

* *In 1915* The Birth of a Nation, *which glorified the Klan, became the first film to be screened at the White House – although Wilson, unhappy with its use of his racist quotes, tried to stop it being shown in wartime.*

Hoover had previously enjoyed cordial relations with African American leaders in the south, and as Secretary of Commerce in Calvin Coolidge's government he had desegregated his department – but now political expediency took over.

- He purged blacks from senior positions in the southern wing of his party

- His campaigners created flyers showing a lustful black man ogling an attractive white secretary to suggest that their Democrat opponent supported interracial relations

Hooverball

Keeping fit isn't easy for a busy president, so the White House doctor, Joel T. Boone, devised a game for Hoover to play with what became known as his 'medicine ball cabinet'.

Hooverball is a cross between volleyball and tennis, with teams hitting a 2.7kg (6lb) medicine ball over a net 24m (8ft) high. A national championship is hosted every year by the Hoover Presidential Library Association and West Branch, Iowa – his birthplace.

- He reacted to a Democrat counter-rumour that he had danced with a black committeewoman by calling it 'indecent and unworthy'

- When a delegation from the Anti-Lynching Congress* delivered a protest to him in 1930, Hoover declined to respond

The New Deal

Hoover had the bad luck to run the country during the Great Depression, and when the next election fell, in 1932, unemployment was running at around 25 per cent. He lost to the Democrats in a landslide.

The victor was the wheelchair-bound governor of New York, Franklin D. Roosevelt, who took office promising the American people a 'New Deal' – and who would become the only president to win four presidential elections.

---

*Research by the Tuskegee Institute found that 4,745 people were lynched between 1882 and 1964, and Southern politicians thwarted anti-lynching laws around 200 times. In June 2018 three black senators introduced a bill in the House which would make lynching a federal hate crime.

FDR, as he was commonly known, launched an ambitious public works programme and shook up the financial system to transform the 'Brother can you spare a dime?' culture.

His Social Security Act established retirement pensions, unemployment insurance and welfare benefits for children in one-parent families, while guaranteeing workers the right to collective bargaining led to a massive rise in union membership.

For African Americans Roosevelt brought a 'new deal' in both policy and practice:

- He was the first president to call out lynching for what it was, describing it as 'a vile form of collective murder'

- He appointed a far greater number of African Americans to senior government posts ('the Black Brains Trust') than any of his predecessors

- He was the first president to appoint an African American as a federal judge, and the first to promote a black man to Brigadier General in the army

'I'm not the smartest fellow in the world, but I can sure pick smart colleagues.'

Franklin D. Roosevelt

Unsung heroine

Frances Perkins, Secretary of Labor from 1933 to 1945, was the first woman ever appointed to a US cabinet. A sociologist and advocate of workers' rights, she was responsible for a wide range of New Deal reforms, including laws against child labour, the introduction of unemployment benefits, the first ever minimum wage and overtime legislation. She also defined the standard 40-hour week.

She arranged for some 400 Jewish refugee children from Nazi Germany to be settled with American families – and remained cool when political opponents* called her a communist, spread a rumour that she was a Russian Jew and even (unsuccessfully) attempted to have her impeached.

* In 2011 the Republican Governor of Maine, Paul LePage, ordered a mural of Perkins to be removed from the state's Department of Labor HQ.

Desegregation

In 1948 Harry S. Truman ended a long-running injustice with his executive order (no. 9981) ruling that 'there shall be equality of treatment and opportunity for all persons in the armed services without regard to race, color, religion or national origin'.

Progress was slow, and when the former war leader Dwight D. Eisenhower took office he stressed his determination to finish the job – although it was in another area that 'Ike' was to make a major stand for racial equality.

In 1957, in defiance of his Civil Rights Act, Orval Faubus, the governor of Arkansas, deployed the National Guard to prevent nine black children enrolling in an all-white school at Little Rock. Eisenhower's response was to send in the Army's 101st Airborne Division (albeit without its black soldiers).

The nine had to suffer a year of verbal and physical abuse before Faubus closed all local schools to avoid desegregation – the so-called Lost Year. Desegregation eventually came to Little Rock, but to continuing white hostility.

- The Public Works Administration inserted a clause in all government contracts fixing a quota for hiring black construction workers

- The National Youth Administration, which employed black supervisors to oversee its work in each state in the South, assisted more than 300,000 African American young people during the Depression

And then another world war came along – and further reforms had to wait.

The Johnson treatment

It was John F. Kennedy's in conception, but after his assassination it was carried through in typical bruising fashion – they called it 'the Johnson treatment' – by his successor in the White House, the canny, manipulative LBJ.

The seminal Civil Rights Act of 1964 – bitterly opposed in the South – outlawed segregation on the grounds of race, religion or national origin in all public places, including parks, courthouses, restaurants, theatres, hotels and sports arenas.

The dogs of war

Kennedy at first took a cautious approach to civil rights legislation, but the violent suppression of black protests in Birmingham, Alabama, in 1963 strengthened his resolve.

Although the population of the city was 40 per cent black, there were no African American policemen, firemen or bank clerks, and there was blatant segregation in public buildings, schools, stores and restaurants.

When schoolchildren marched in protest – and as the world looked on – the city's commissioner of public safety, Eugene 'Bull' Connor, ordered the use of fire hoses and attack dogs against them. Hundreds of youngsters were arrested.

Within weeks local business leaders defused the situation, upgrading the jobs of blacks and desegregating lunch counters, restrooms, fitting rooms and drinking fountains at department stores.

'The civil rights movement should thank God for Bull Connor,' Kennedy is reported to have said. 'He's helped it as much as Abraham Lincoln.'

It also banned discrimination on the same grounds by employers and trade unions, and had several meaningful kicks in its tail:

- It created an Equal Employment Opportunity Commission empowered to file lawsuits on behalf of aggrieved workers

- It forbade the use of federal funds for any discriminatory programmes

- It authorised what is now the Department of Education to assist with school desegregation

- It prohibited the unequal application of voting requirements

The civil rights leader Martin Luther King, himself soon to be assassinated, hailed it as 'a second emancipation'.

Johnson argued for the legislation to be passed as a lasting legacy to the martyred president, but he had to overcome fierce opposition in Congress. A filibuster by southern senators held the bill up for a full 75 days until – tirelessly lobbying and working the phones – he at last corralled the votes he needed.

When he signed the Act into law in the East Room on July 2nd, 1964,* Johnson used 72 ceremonial pens which would later be given as mementoes to backers of the most far-reaching civil rights legislation in the nation's history.

In a televised address to the people (one of the greatest political speeches of modern times) he uttered a ringing challenge: 'We have come to a time of testing. We must not fail.'

Heartbreak motel

The Act was itself soon tested – in a Supreme Court case brought by the 216-room Heart of Atlanta Motel, Georgia, which had always refused to let its rooms to blacks.

Its owner, Moreton Rolleston, argued that the law violated the Fifth Amendment, which allowed him to run his business as he liked, and (the ultimate irony) that forcing him to admit clients he didn't want put him in a position of 'involuntary servitude'.

---

* It was nine years to the day since, as a 60-a-day smoker, he had suffered a near-fatal heart attack.

The unanimous 9–0 ruling against the motel, albeit it that the judgement concentrated on commercial clauses in the Act, effectively put an end, once and for all, to the discriminatory Jim Crow laws of the South.

Legacy

Like the UK's Tony Blair decades later, his liberal achievements overshadowed by the debacle of the Iraq War, so Johnson's civil rights triumph has, for many critics, been outweighed by the US involvement in Vietnam.

A genuine moral gift to the nation it was, however, and one with consequences the seasoned politico well understood from the beginning.

'We have lost the South for a generation,' he's said to have remarked to a Democrat aide – and so they had.

'If I did not rise with dignity, I can at least fall with ease, which is the more difficult task.'

CHAPTER fIVE

ALL THE PRESIDENTS' WOMEN

She's never had an officially defined role, and she isn't paid for what she does, but the First Lady has her own staff in the East Wing and, whether she likes it or not, finds herself continuously in the public eye.

If, by long tradition, her prime task has been organising the White House social round and glad-handing the consorts of distinguished guests, many a FLOTUS has bridled at the 'dutiful wife' expectation – while a fascinating few have stepped out of the shadows to make a mark in their own right.

fLOTUS stand-ins 1

When a president doesn't have a wife to hand, someone else has to step up to the plate...

Thomas Jefferson was a widower when he became president. He invited Dolley Madison (the wife of his secretary of state) to act as his hostess, but occasionally his daughter Patsy played the role. In 1806, during her second visit, she gave birth to her eighth child, James Madison Randolph – who thus became the first baby to be born in the White House.

Andrew Jackson followed the wishes of his late wife Rachel in having her niece Emily Donelson as his hostess. She later shared the post with their daughter-in-law Sara.

Martin Van Buren, also a widower, chose a First Lady whose extravagance led to his failure to win a second term. Angelica Singleton was just 22 when she married Van Buren's son Abraham. The couple had a lengthy honeymoon tour of Europe, after which she introduced the airs and graces of the French court to the White House. This provoked the devastatingly witty 'Gold Spoon oration' in the House by the Whig Charles Ogle, which damaged Van Buren's reputation.

Martha Washington, the first to take on the responsibility, wasn't at all happy with it, not least because one of the rules imposed on the presidential couple was that they weren't allowed to accept private invitations into people's homes.

A riotous pen

She apparently just got on with the job, whereas her successor, **Abigail Adams**, was the first real grouch of a First Lady – and who could blame her?

We'd call her a feminist today. She was well educated and opinionated. Even as her husband and his rebel friends planned the new country's first constitution, she argued they should seize the opportunity to create a government giving women equal status to men.

When he got the top job she feared that her free-thinking days were over. 'My pen runs riot,' she wrote to Adams. 'I forget that it must grow cautious and prudent. I fear I shall make a dull business when such restrictions are placed upon it.'

In another letter she described the First Lady role as like being 'fastened up hand and foot and tongue to be shot at as our Quincy lads [her mother's family] do at the poor geese and turkies'.

But Abigail was too feisty for that. In those turbulent political times she couldn't help speaking her mind. Face to face with Alexander Hamilton she told him she was looking 'into the eyes of the devil himself'.

In a spat with an anti-federalist opponent she called him 'the sly, the artful, the insidious [Albert] Gallatin', and he replied by dubbing her 'Mrs President' – a sarcastic title that stuck.

Did she mind very much? We see her stopping off on a journey home* to inspect a New Jersey federal army camp and even review the troops, before admitting to her husband a little coyly: 'I acted as your proxy.'

---

* Home was only briefly the newly built White House. She arrived in November 1800, spending four months there as the first First Lady in residence – and hanging out her washing to dry in the unfinished East Room.

By the time it was all over, though, she was 'sick, sick, sick of public life' and, in a letter to her son, wrote a kind of First Lady epitaph: 'If I did not rise with dignity, I can at least fall with ease, which is the more difficult task.'

The Presidentress

Dolley Madison was much happier in the role. After two terms managing the White House entertainments for Thomas Jefferson (*page 124*), she now had another two on her husband's watch, and she was such a visible and influential presence that she was often referred to as Lady Madison and even (good naturedly) the Presidentress.

In her trademark turban, and wearing striking, low-cut dresses, she set a standard for those future First Ladies (by no means all of them) who would enjoy making a mark in public life. She was prominent in fundraising activities to support the Lewis and Clark expedition, and she involved herself in charities – helping to found a home for orphaned girls in Washington DC, for instance, and forging links with the nuns in a local Catholic school.

Dolley Maddison lived to the age of 81, by which time she was the living embodiment of the Founding Fathers era* (and often called on to reminisce about it), while her home in Philadelphia, with its collection of portraits, letters and other paraphernalia, had become a kind of museum of the period.

There was, though, a sadness at the end. Her husband, whom she had outlived by 13 years, had failed to reveal the extent of their son Payne's alcohol-fuelled gambling habit, and this brought her close to ruin.

The bigamous wife

Politics can be a dirty business, and it's perhaps not surprising that Andrew Jackson's bigamous marriage should be used against him in his 1828 presidential campaign. He never forgave his opponent for what happened next.

She was so loved a national figure that when, in 1844, the Morse Code inventor Samuel Morse demonstrated his new invention in Washington, the 76-year-old Dolley was invited to send the very first message by a private citizen.

The facts about the first, failed marriage of the young **Rachel Jackson** were fiercely contested. Her family said she fled from her husband, Lewis Robards, because he ill-treated her; his family that he threw her out of the house because of her flirtations.

What is beyond question is that, thinking she had been divorced, she went through an illegal marriage ceremony with Jackson.

They were properly married well before Jackson ran for president, and by then she was every bit the pious Christian, but newspapers supporting the candidacy of John Quincy Adams were merciless in portraying her as a bigamist and a divorcee.

'Ought a convicted adulteress and her paramour husband,' trumpeted one editorial, *'to be placed in the highest offices of this free and Christian land?'*

These attacks didn't prevent Jackson winning the contest, but the shaming seems to have exacerbated Rachel's poor health – and she died in the period between his election and the inauguration.

FLOTUS stand-ins 2

Anna Harrison never entered the White House with her husband – not from any cussedness, but because she was ill at the time of his inauguration and he died before she had recovered. Her daughter-in-law Jane Harrison deputised, accompanied by her father's elderly sister, Jane Findlay.

John Tyler's wife Letitia was the first First Lady to die in the White House. Their daughter-in-law Priscilla, a vivacious actress, assumed her duties and entertained guests as varied as Charles Dickens and Napoleon's family. When she moved away, the Tylers' 23-year-old daughter Letty took over, but within three months the president had married someone her own age, Julia Gardiner. Letty was mortified, and she refused to have any dealings with her new mother-in-law.

As Zachary Taylor was a natural scarecrow, his wife Peggy took care of his wardrobe, but she was something of a recluse and refused to busy herself with entertaining visitors. Their daughter, Betty Bliss (addressed as Miss Betty), became the official face at public functions – so successfully that the composer Charles Grobe wrote a polka in her honour.

'May God Almighty forgive her murderers,' Jackson said. 'I never can.'

The tender epitaph he wrote for Rachel describes her as 'a being so gentle and so virtuous,* slander might wound but could not dishonor.'

Lincoln blues

Few presidents' wives can have had such a tough time as **Mary Todd Lincoln**. Since she came from Kentucky stock, she was accused by northerners of being sympathetic to the Confederacy and by southerners of being a traitor to the cause.

Within a year of entering the White House the couple lost their 11-year-old son Willie to typhoid fever, while many of her friends and family in the South died in the civil war.

---

* And heroic. She was the legal guardian for six boys and two girls, and she also adopted two boys – one of them, Lyncoya, a Native American found by Jackson on a battlefield with his dead mother, and raised by the couple from the age of two.

Refurbishing the White House at great cost (to enhance the reputation of the presidency and the Union, she would say) brought her both ridicule and condemnation, while in 1863 she was thrown from her carriage and knocked unconscious.

The assassination of her husband would deal her the ultimate blow, but even before that abrupt shock she was said to be suffering from acute depression.

Despite her anguish and all the tensions of the Civil War, it should be said, she continued to function. She worked as a volunteer nurse in Union hospitals, reviewed the troops with the president and – as an ardent abolitionist – regarded the Emancipation Proclamation as a personal triumph.

Through her friendship with her dressmaker, Elizabeth Hobbs Keckley, she was involved in the Contraband Relief Association which raised private donations to house, clothe and give medical treatment to recently freed slaves. (Keckley, herself a former slave, would later write an intimate autobiography.)

fLOTUS stand-ins 3

The novelist Nathaniel Hawthorne described Franklin Pierce's wife Jane as 'that death's head' in the White House – but the poor woman had plenty to be depressed about. She had already lost two of her three sons when, shortly before her husband's inauguration, they and their 12-year-old Benny were in a railway carriage which came off the tracks and plunged down an embankment. The adults survived with minor injuries, but Benny was killed instantly. Pierce, believing he had been punished by God for past sins, refused to swear on the Bible during his inauguration, while Jane understandably had no heart for White House activities (she spent hours writing letters to her dead son) and arranged for a series of other women, including the wives of cabinet ministers, to take her place.

James Buchanan was the only president to remain a lifelong bachelor, and his young niece Harriet Lane acted as his hostess. She was apparently better at socialising than managing household affairs: Buchanan wasn't above sometimes criticising her in public for the quality of the food served up at formal dinners.

Traumatised first by Lincoln's death, and years later by the sudden death of another son, Tad, Mary was in 1875 committed to a lunatic asylum in Illinois, where she twice tried to take her own life.

Later discharged, she lived in France for some time, eventually dying at her sister's home in Springfield, Illinois, in 1882.

A magnetic failure

In 1872 the suffragist Victoria Woodhull was the first woman to run for President, 'self-nominated' by the Equal Rights Party she had founded and adopting the black abolitionist Frederick Douglass as her running mate.

A colourful advocate of free love, who had made a first fortune by taking to the road as a 'magnetic healer' and a second by becoming a stockbroker, she spent election day in jail, facing a charge of obscenity.

A few months short of her 35th birthday, she would have been too young to enter the White House had she won – but, alas, she didn't receive a single electoral vote.

Bedazzled

We've become used to a touch of glamour among First Ladies in recent times, but the first to catch the public attention for her star quality was **Frances Cleveland**. In June 1886, at the age of 21,* she married her deceased father's friend Grover, the grizzled 49-year-old widower and Republican president who had known her as a baby.

The only First Lady to be married in the White House, she remains the youngest ever presidential wife.

Dubbed 'Frankie' by the press – a usage she disliked, although she'd originally been named Frank after an uncle – she was an instant hit.

Young women adopted her distinctive hairstyle and her low-cut gowns (to the horror of the Women's Christian Temperance Union), while businesses shamelessly used her image in advertisements to promote a huge range of products that had nothing to do with her at all.

---

* *She missed his inauguration ceremony because she wasn't allowed to take time off from her college studies.*

fLOTUS stand-ins 4

Andrew Johnson's wife Eliza, stricken by the death of their son Charles in a riding accident, knew how to martial her emotional resources. She was happy to play the front-of-house hostess at formal dinners, but she delegated lesser events to her daughters, Martha Patterson and Mary Stover.

Chester Arthur's wife died shortly before his presidency, and he at first decided to make do with the wives and daughters of his cabinet ministers. Eventually, however, he co-opted his sister Molly McElroy, and although she had no experience of such a daunting job, she soon grew into it – and 3,000 admirers packed into the White House for her last public reception.

Towards the end of her stint, Molly became good friends with Elizabeth Cleveland, the unmarried sister of the man who would soon succeed her brother as president. Chester Cleveland entered office as a bachelor, and Elizabeth fulfilled the hostess role before his marriage to Frances Folsom – so that (it's never happened before or since) the stand-in duties were consecutively carried out by presidents' sisters.

While steering clear of party politics, she was very much a feminist in the roles she chose to play.

- She hosted receptions on Saturday mornings for working-class women who couldn't visit the White House during the week

- She attended the launch of an organisation promoting educational opportunities for factory workers, her mingling with women workers making the cover of *Harper's Weekly*

- She encouraged the careers of young women musicians – and a violinist she sponsored to study in Berlin became the first American to win the Mendelssohn Stipendium

- She helped individual women to pursue a college degree and professional employment

- Having encountered two starving girls eating out of a garbage can, she helped an African American woman found The Washington Home for Friendless Colored Girls

- She was actively involved in the Colored Christmas Club charity, providing food and clothing to poor local children

After her husband lost the 1888 election, Frances Cleveland is said to have told the White House staff to look after the place for them, as they'd be back in four years' time – which they were, becoming the only couple to serve non-consecutive terms.

Modern times

Edith Roosevelt wasn't deeply involved in political affairs, but when her husband Teddy won the Nobel Peace Prize in 1906 for negotiating the end of the Russo-Japanese War, much of the credit was hers: she had acted as a secret conduit between the president and their friend, the British chargé d'affaires in St. Petersburg (and later US ambassador) Cecil Spring-Rice.

Her practical legacy was the modernisation of the White House administration, creating the first full-time, salaried staff. She also oversaw the revamping of the building's interior after the creation of the new West Wing. Out went fuddy-duddy Victorian features, to be replaced by 'colonial revival' furnishings, giving a cleaner, brighter look.

As for the newly fashioned East Wing through which visitors entered, she had the walls of the hall lined with portraits of past presidential wives and hostesses, together with dinner service plates used by previous First Ladies.

Naughty girl

Theodore Roosevelt's first wife died in childbirth, and his daughter Alice was brought up alongside the five children he had with his second wife, Edith. Alice became known for her wildness: smoking, gambling, partying – and keeping a pet snake named Emily Spinach.

Roosevelt is reported to have said in despair: 'I can either run the country or I can attend to Alice, but I can't possibly do both.'

She married the Republican politician Nicholas Longworth, but campaigned against him in an election, had several affairs and gave birth to an illegitimate child after a fling with a senator.

When it was time to leave the White House she buried a voodoo doll of the incoming First Lady, Nellie Taft, under the lawn.

Cherry blossom time

The spirited **Nellie Taft** had the cruel luck to suffer a stroke soon after her husband became president (she temporarily lost the power of speech), but she still made a significant mark during her time at the White House.

She struck an early visible blow for African Americans by replacing the all-white ushers who greeted visitors in the East Wing (a prestigious job) with uniformed black staff.

She was the first hostess to introduce the now customary musical entertainment after state dinners, she lifted an existing block on divorced people being invited to official events and she faced down abolitionists who wanted her to ban alcohol from the tables.

A few more of Nellie's FLOTUS firsts:

- The first to openly support women's suffrage
- The first to lobby for safety stands in federal workplaces
- The first to own and drive a car
- The first to smoke cigarettes in public

She would also later become the first presidential wife to write her memoirs, *Recollection of Full Years*.

Her most lasting legacy is the scintillating spring display of cherry blossom in what is now West Potomac Park. Dazzled by a similar pink-and-white flowering in Luneta Park, Manila, while Taft was serving as governor-general of the Philippines, she arranged for 3,000 Japanese cherries (*sakura*) to be introduced to the tidal basin and in the grounds of the Capitol.

flOTUS stand-ins 5

After Woodrow Wilson's first wife Ellen died a year into his first term, their 28-year-old daughter Margaret, a professional singer, took over the running of the White House with the help of Wilson's cousin, Helen Bones. Margaret was unmarried, and persistent unfounded newspaper rumours about her love life so annoyed Wilson that he wrote a severe note to the White House Press Corps, with the aggressive, sleeves-rolled-up final line: 'If this continues I shall deal with you, not as President, but as man to man.'

De facto president?

There was no playing the traditional role for **Edith Wilson**. Having married the widowed Woodrow almost two years into his first term, she would soon be managing a White House shorn of its regular entertainments during the First World War, and then – with the conflict over – facing the task of keeping the ship of state afloat during the last eighteen months of his presidency after he was partially paralysed by a stroke.

In the years leading up to the war she annoyed Wilson's trusted advisor Edmund House by sitting in on discussions with politicians and foreign diplomats, and the president later even gave her access to a secret wartime code.

During the war she set an example by observing gasless Sundays (garaging the cars), meatless Mondays and wheatless Wednesdays. She raised funds for the Red Cross by selling wool from sheep grazing on the White House lawn, and (unsqueamishly) released a public service warning to soldiers about the dangers of contracting VD while serving abroad.

She later raised the profile of the First Lady by accompanying Wilson, and so mixing with European queens and other royalty,* when he signed the Treaty of Versailles in 1919.

But did she run a bedside government after his stroke, as many historians believe? This was her take on it: 'I studied every paper sent from the different secretaries or senators, and tried to digest and present in tabloid form the things that, despite my vigilance, had to go to the President.

'I, myself, never made a single decision regarding the disposition of public affairs.'

She did, though, contrive to keep Congress and the nation at large in the dark about Wilson's condition during what she called her 'stewardship'. Acting as the conduit between her husband and his cabinet, she scribbled notes which they had to accept were the sick president's instructions, taken down verbatim.

---

* She was immensely proud of a supposed descent from the Native American princess Pocahontas, though the amount of shared blood amounted to a thimbleful.

The first Lady of the World

In **Eleanor Roosevelt*** we meet a giant among
First Ladies. As her reputation derives from a
tirelessly influential career in support of civil
rights and social reform, it's not surprising
that she attracted enemies, but in 1999 Gallup
ranked her ninth in a list of 'the most widely
admired people of the 20th century'.

Truman called her 'The First Lady of the World'.

She didn't always agree with her husband – she
and FDR sometimes resembled stars wheeling
in separate firmaments – and she would never
have entered the White House at all had she
made a different decision when discovering his
affair with Lucy Mercer (*page 165*).

As it was, she served for a record twelve years
through the Depression and the Second World
War, and continued to make an impact on
national and world affairs for years afterwards.

---

* *She was actually born a Roosevelt – the niece of Theodore and the fifth
cousin once removed of her husband, Franklin.*

A strong-minded intellectual who always did things her own way, she was happy to meet the public and argue her case. She wrote a column entitled 'I Want You to Write to Me' for *Women's Home Companion* magazine, asking readers for their opinions, and 300,000 responded in the first five months. (She gave her fees to charities.)

Her personal, generally light-hearted 'My Day' column was syndicated around the country; she wrote magazine articles for a variety of magazines; and she's reckoned to have given some 1,400 speeches, usually from notes.

Mines of information

Few bookshelves boast a copy of the medieval work *De re metallica*, a study of metal mining, refining and smelting, but it earns a place here because of the names on the cover of the first English version, published in London in 1912 by public subscription.

The translators were the future White House couple Herbert Hoover (a mining engineer) and his First Lady, Lou (a geologist).

No caged bird

Washington was a racially segregated city in 1939, and the Daughters of the American Revolution (DAR) refused permission for the celebrated African American contralto Marian Anderson to perform at a concert in its Constitution Hall.

Eleanor Roosevelt, who had invited Anderson to sing at the White House years before, was a member of DAR. She highlighted the issue in her 'My Day' newspaper column: 'To remain as a member implies approval of that action; therefore I am resigning.' *

The First Lady went further, however – working behind the scenes to help organise an Easter Sunday outdoor concert at the Lincoln Memorial that was also broadcast by radio networks across the country. A racially diverse crowd of 75,000 heard Anderson sing operatic numbers in the first half of the concert and negro spirituals in the second, ending with 'Nobody Knows the Trouble I've Seen'.

* Six years later her successor Bess Truman did accept a DAR invitation, the subsequent furore leading to the overturning of its segregation policy.

And then there were her radio shows. She made hundreds of broadcasts, for which she was paid by the advertisers of everything from coffee, beauty soap and cold cream to typewriters and building materials. To the criticism that this was demeaning, she shrugged that it was a good way to raise money for her causes.

The press conferences she gave in the early days had an unusual feature: in order to help women reporters keep their jobs during the Depression she imposed a ban on male journalists. When women were excluded from the hacks' annual Gridiron Dinner she promptly established the Gridiron Widows – and held the event at the White House.

She somehow found the time to write several books during her incumbency. The jauntily titled *It's Up to the Women* was a buck-up to her own sex in hard times, while *This Troubled World* and *The Moral Basis of Democracy* looked ahead to the rigours of a possible war. She also wrote children's fiction and *This is My Story*, the best-selling first volume of what would become a triple-decker autobiography.

> 'What other single human being
> has touched and transformed the
> existence of so many?'
>
> *US diplomat Adlai Stevenson*

A few typical Eleanor Roosevelt initiatives:

- She sponsored White House conferences, on such topics as the needs of unemployed women and the participation of black women and children in federal welfare programmes

- She ensured that African-Americans were beneficiaries of New Deal programmes – and ignored the inevitable criticisms

- She helped rehouse impoverished coal-mining families in West Virginia, insisting that the new homes were equipped with modern facilities

- She encouraged FDR to issue an executive order which banned employment discrimination on 'race, creed, color or national origin'

After her White House tenure was over, she was appointed as one of the five US delegates to the newly formed United Nations.

The giving impulse

It was an impossible act to follow, and **Bess Truman** didn't try. She hated the trappings of being a president's wife, ditched press conferences and when a camera came close would, in the words of Truman's biographer David McCullough, 'become kind of Old Stoneface, and get an expression that looked as if her feet hurt'.

Down to earth

We can't resist a popular story about Harry S. Truman,* known for his plain-speaking. Touring a farming area, he's said to have given a speech in which he stressed the importance of spreading the fields with manure.

'Bess, dear,' implored a friend, 'can't you get him to call it fertiliser?'

'You don't know,' came the reply, 'how many years it's taken me to get him to say manure.'

Americans love using an initial, but Truman's was just that: he didn't have a middle name.

One thing she *was* happy to do was sponsor charities and host meetings for them in the White House – and after the Second World War she gave her name to initiatives by the Girl Scouts to relieve the suffering of children in Europe and Japan.

In fact, using their privileged First Lady position to promote good causes has become a feature of White House hostesses, both during their tenure and in retirement.

After her husband suffered a heart attack while in office, **Mamie Eisenhower** (herself a smoker) chaired fundraising drives by the American Heart Association. She also backed the building of a retirement home for Army widows on a 16-acre site in Washington DC.

Lady Bird Johnson fostered a programme to provide underprivileged pre-school children with education skills and basic medical care and nutrition. She's best remembered, though, for the national wildflower centre at the University of Texas (now named after her), to which she originally donated 60 acres of her own land.

Home improvements

As soon as she arrived in the White House the artistic and fashionable **Jackie Kennedy** set up a committee of experts on paintings, furniture and books with the aim of restoring its public rooms.*

From the French minister of Culture, Andre Malraux (who agreed to send Leonardo da Vinci's Mona Lisa from the Louvre across the Atlantic on loan) she devised the idea of creating a department of arts and humanities for the US – and it's in this area that she would probably have made her greatest contribution had her time as First Lady not been so cruelly cut short.

Five years after the assassination she married her old friend, the Greek shipping magnate Aristotle Onassis. Although she lived abroad for much of the year, she involved herself in several cultural conservation projects in the US – using her influence, for instance, to help save Grand Central Station in New York from demolition by developers.

* *Discovering that previous occupants had walked off with many of the furnishings, she initiated a bill in Congress to make them national property.*

Pat Nixon, who helped bring a vast collection of art and furnishings to the White House, made volunteerism her chief charitable cause – encouraging people to address social problems locally through offering their help at hospitals, rehabilitation centres and the like.

No First Lady was more open about her own problems than **Betty Ford**. She raised breast cancer awareness after having a mastectomy, and then admitted a long-running personal history of alcoholism and substance abuse – later founding the Betty Ford Centre to help those with similar problems. She also (to unease among some fellow Republicans) declared herself for feminism, equal rights and gun control.

Setting up a mental health council was **Rosalynn Carter**'s priority, a target she achieved during her husband's single term of office.

Nancy Reagan led a campaign against drugs, with the slogan 'Just say no' – and saw drug and alcohol addiction fall significantly during the mid-Eighties.

Barbara Bush was the inspiration behind the National Literacy Act of 1991, while her eponymous Foundation for Family Literacy directs its funds towards pre-school children and their parents.

A former librarian, **Laura Bush** followed in her mother-in-law's footsteps with her 'Ready to Read, Ready to Learn' literacy programme for the very young.

Michelle Obama's 'Let's Move' was designed to tackle childhood obesity – and she developed a vegetable plot in the White House garden to demonstrate healthy things to eat.

Melania Trump launched her 'Be Best' public awareness campaign to promote well-being among young people, with a special focus on cyberbullying and opioid use.

And **Hillary Clinton**? We'll come across her charitable foundation in the next chapter, which finds American presidents – and sometimes their wives – mired in unfortunate controversies . . .

'I did not have sexual
relations with that
woman'

CHAPTER SIX

CONDUCT UNBECOMING

None of us is without fault, but when presidents go off the rails there's nowhere to hide. If their sins aren't immediately plastered all over the news media, to a chorus of mingled disgust and glee, be sure that eager historians will later dig and delve to bring every last failing into the glare of day.

Having dealt with their record on slavery and racial segregation, we now turn the spotlight on sins great and small which have set tongues wagging – among them bribery, corruption and, of course, sexual incontinence.

155

If contempt and ridicule are hard enough to bear, the threat of impeachment* hangs over those suspected of serious offences (specifically 'treason, bribery or other high crimes and misdemeanors') – the tally so far being two cases taken all the way and one narrowly avoided.

Tribune of the people

Andrew Johnson was always angling for a battle with Congress. As we've seen (*page 106*), he took over as president after Lincoln's assassination and, as a Tennessee Democrat, was opposed to punishing measures the majority Republicans wanted to inflict on the defeated South.

In 1866, after Congress overturned his vetoes on civil rights legislation, he took to the road on an 18-day 'Swing Around the Circle' speaking tour, promoting himself as a populist 'tribune of the people'.

Impeachment leads to a trial by the Senate, with a two-thirds majority required to 'convict' the president and force his resignation.

It was a disaster. Comparing himself to Jesus Christ in his willingness to forgive repentant sinners, he engaged in shouting matches with hecklers, and when his handlers tried to calm him down defiantly replied 'I don't care about my dignity!' – a comment duly reported in newspapers across the nation.

In Indianapolis there were gunfights between his supporters and their opponents, while in Pennsylvania hundreds of spectators plunged 6m (20ft) into a drained canal when improvised staging by a railway track collapsed.

As Johnson had been visibly drunk during his inauguration as vice president a year before, his enemies were quick to blame his wild behaviour and intemperate language on the bottle.

'It is mortifying,' winced an editorial in the previously sympathetic *New York Herald* , 'to see a man occupying the lofty position of President of the United States descend from that position and join issue with those who are dragging their garments in the muddy gutters of political vituperation.'

The crunch came when, in bold defiance of Congress, he sacked the Secretary of War, Edwin Stanton. In March 1868 the House approved ten 'articles of impeachment', which included dismissing Stanton and making three speeches in an attempt 'to bring into disgrace, ridicule, hatred, contempt and reproach, the Congress of the United States'.

The senate voted 35–19 against him – just one vote short of what was needed for conviction. He had lived to fight another day.

Watergate

'Tricky Dicky' is the name his enemies gave Richard Nixon – and that was well before the affair which lent the suffix *-gate* to many a subsequent scandal.

In June 1972 five 'burglars' were caught breaking into the Democratic National Committee's HQ in the Watergate office complex in Washington DC. It took some enterprising newspaper reporting to uncover the shocking truth: they'd been sent there by the Nixon administration to bug the building.

Before the opening of what became a furiously threshing can of worms (with 49 government officials indicted or jailed), Nixon had won a landslide election victory. He now pulled every trick he knew to cover up a slew of illegal activities, including the break-in, the paying of 'hush money', the bugging of political opponents and the use of the FBI and the CIA to investigate his rivals.

Nixon in China

The visit of the arch anti-communist President Richard Nixon to Beijing in 1972 was a political shock which would later become a cultural one.

Nixon's initiative, brokered by his National Security Advisor Henry Kissinger, brought a welcome thaw in chilly East-West relations.

In 1987 the composer John Adams and the librettist Alice Goodman premiered their opera* *Nixon in China* in Houston – and it has since become a fixture in the repertoire.

* *Nixon was himself a musician. He played the piano, violin, clarinet, saxophone and accordion, and even wrote a piano concerto.*

All the President's Men

The two determined young *Washington Post* reporters who broke the Watergate story, Bob Woodward and Carl Bernstein, published their devastating account of the scandal, *All the President's Men*, two months before Nixon resigned. (It was later turned into a film of the same name, starring Robert Redford and Dustin Hoffman.) The former New York Times managing editor Gene Roberts described their work as 'maybe the single greatest reporting effort of all time'.

House of Cards

The long-running TV series *House of Cards* began life as a trilogy of political thrillers by the British Conservative politician Michael Dobbs, later turned into a BBC mini series between 1989 and 1994. The ruthless power play of the American Netflix version, which first appeared in 2013 and ran until 2018, was inspired by Watergate-type skulduggery. Its leading character, the Democrat Frank Underwood (played by Kevin Spacey until the final season), rises to the presidency, and then becomes First Gentleman when his wife, Claire (Robin Wright), gets the top job.

His undoing was the tape-recording system he had installed in his offices, revealing how much he knew. On the night of August 7, 1974, a group of senior Republican politicians arrived in the Oval Office to tell Nixon that his impeachment was inevitable – and the following evening, in order to avoid it, he gave a TV address announcing his resignation.

A month later his successor, Gerald Ford, issued a full and unconditional pardon.

A stained dress

'I did not have sexual relations with that woman,' Bill Clinton declared in January 1998, standing alongside his wife Hillary at a White House press conference. 'These allegations are false.'

The woman in question was a former White House intern, Monica Lewinsky. Not only were the allegations true, but Clinton had also made a more thorough denial of his behaviour in a sworn deposition – and this would lead to his impeachment that December on the grounds of perjury and obstruction of justice.

'Monicagate' (as some have styled it) arose from the allegation by a former Arkansas state employee, Paula Jones, that Clinton had sexually harrassed her. They eventually settled out of court – costing him $850,000 (£660,000) – but not before Jones had claimed that he had a history of improper behaviour with women, and her lawyers had homed in on the Lewinsky relationship to prove it.

Solid foundation?

The Bill, Hillary and [daughter] Chelsea Foundation undoubtedly does excellent charitable work around the world, with an annual budget of well over $200 million (£155 million) spent on liberal causes – so why has it been so controversial?

When Hillary Clinton ran for president in 2016 her opponents were quick to suggest that rich donors (some of them with doubtful reputations) were in effect buying influence. Although she signed a document promising to keep her political campaign separate from her charitable work, and although Charity Watch has given the Foundation an 'A' rating, the criticisms have never gone away.

Unfortunately for Clinton one of Lewinsky's friends had not only taped her account of performing oral sex on the President in the White House, but had advised her to keep a semen-stained dress in her wardrobe as evidence.

The game was up!

Impeachment, though, provides a high bar for senators to jump. Conviction required 67 of them to vote against Clinton, but the numbers were only 45 on the perjury charge and 50 on obstruction of justice. He, too, had wriggled free.

Many a *slip*

Exposure may be more unforgiving in our multimedia age, but more than a third of US presidents down the ages have been involved in sexual improprieties of one kind or another.

- **Four early presidents are thought to have fathered children by their slaves: George Washington (good grief!), Thomas Jefferson, William Henry Harrison and John Tyler.**

- Ten years before his election, Grover Cleveland had a son, Oscar, by a 38-year-old widow, Maria Halpin, who claimed that he had forced himself on her. The boy was given the middle name Folson after the old friend whose daughter Cleveland would marry while in the White House (page 135), and Maria was briefly, and illegally, incarcerated in a lunatic asylum.

During the 1884 campaign Cleveland's opponents repeatedly catcalled him with the derisory chant, 'Ma, ma – where's my pa?'

- Warren Harding, who in letters to one of his mistresses fondly called his member Jerry, fathered a daughter with the young Nan Britton while in office, and over a period of several years had sex with her in the White House – often, she wrote in a kiss-and-tell book after his death, in 'a closet in the ante-room, evidently a place for hats and coats'.

She had lost her virginity to him in a New York hotel when he was 50 and she just 20: 'I remember so well I wore a pink linen dress which was rather short and enhanced the little-girl look.'

- In September 1918 Eleanor Roosevelt was unpacking her husband's luggage when she discovered letters revealing his passionate love affair with her secretary Lucy Rutherfurd. (She destroyed them.)

During the inevitable bruising confrontation that followed, FDR agreed to break off the romance – though it would last all his life – and the couple were persuaded by his dominating mother that it would be a social and political disaster to get divorced.

Gun *law*

Duelling was commonplace in the South before the Civil War, and Andrew Jackson is said to have settled several disputes this way.

In 1806 he issued a challenge to Charles Dickinson, who had called his wife Rachel a bigamist and accused him of being a coward after they had a disagreement about a horse racing bet. Jackson took a bullet in the chest (the wound would trouble him all his life), but shot Dickinson dead.

Eleanor, who told a daughter that sex with her husband was 'an ordeal to be borne', was to find an overpowering love of her own* – for the whisky drinking, cigarette smoking, female Press Association reporter Lorena Hickok, popularly known as Hick.

One of Hick's erotic letters to her remembered 'the feeling of that soft spot just north-east of the corner of your mouth against my lips'.

- **The mild-mannered golf fanatic Dwight Eisenhower (he played some 800 rounds while in office, and had a putting green installed in the White House grounds) enjoyed a close relationship with his driver Kay Summersby during the Second World War – although a full sexual consummation has never been proved.**

She later wrote of the time when they suddenly found themselves in one another's arms: 'Our ties came off, our buttons were unbuttoned, it was as if we were frantic. And we were.'

---

* She also had a close relationship with the aviator Amelia Earhart which led to her acquiring a student pilot permit – but FDR forbade her to fly.

- John F. Kennedy was an ardent womaniser, who confided in the grandfatherly UK prime minister Harold Macmillan, 'If I don't have a woman for three days I get a terrible headache.'

Tongues wagged about his relationship with Marilyn Monroe after she sang a schmoozy song to him at a public birthday celebration, but the fact is that his aides ferried a bustling succession of women, both famous and unknown, to his bed – and it's a wonder that his headache theory was ever put to the test.

Perhaps because he took a wide range of drugs for his health problems, his staying power was said to be weak. His wife Jackie told a friend that 'he goes too fast and falls asleep', while the actress Angie Dickinson described her tumble with him as 'the best 20 seconds of my life'.

- That old roué Lyndon Johnson, who had several affairs during his marriage, seems to have felt bested by the prodigious skirt-chasing of the younger man.

'I've had more women by accident,' he once growled, 'than Kennedy ever had on purpose.'

Eugenics

We've already observed Woodrow Wilson's racism. It was founded in part on a warped interpretation of the 'survival of the fittest' element in the evolutionary theories of Charles Darwin. He believed, in short, in eugenics – the pseudo science that regarded some races as superior to others and would soon lead to the horrors of Hitler's human experiments in his prison camps.

The closest Wilson got to putting his ideas into practice was in 1911, when as governor of New Jersey he signed a bill into legislation which allowed the forcible sterilisation of criminals and 'feeble-minded' adults. He set up a board of examiners to decide who should be treated – but the law was struck down within two years as unconstitutional.

Teapot Dome

What's been called 'the greatest and most sensational scandal in the history of American politics' – before Watergate, that is – occurred on Warren Harding's watch.

Nobody ever suggested that Harding personally took a cut, but the bribery case blackened his administration and his name along with it.

His Interior Secretary, Albert Fall, had leased Navy oil reserves at Teapot Dome in Wyoming to private companies at a low rate and without any competitive bidding. As with Watergate, investigators 'followed the money' – which they found had gone to his cattle ranch and other business interests.

In 1929 Fall was convicted of taking bribes, and became the first member of a US presidential cabinet ever to be jailed.

Iran-Contra

What connection could there possibly be for the US between Iran in the distant Middle East and Nicaragua in its own backyard?

The answer during Ronald Reagan's time at the White House was that money illegally raised through arm sales to one of the countries was used to provide illegal shipments of arms to the other. Yes, another scandal . . .

A few curiosities

- John Quincy Adams enjoyed a naked swim in the Potomac every morning.

- Ulysses S. Grant smoked 20 cigars a day – and died of throat cancer.

- James A. Garfield was ambidextrous, and could write Latin with one hand while writing Greek with the other.

- Grover Cleveland was called The Buffalo Hangman by his political opponents because, while sheriff of Erie County, he had twice personally operated the noose mechanism to execute murderers.

- George W. Bush is the only president to have run a marathon, clocking a time of 3:44:52 at Houston, eight years before his inauguration, at the age of 46.

- Barack Obama's high school nickname on the basketball team was 'Barry O'Bomber' because of his remarkable jump shot.

Although the administration later claimed that its motive for covertly breaking the embargo on arming Iran (via Israel) was a trade-off for the release of American hostages in Lebanon, a congressional investigation revealed that the sales had begun a year before the first hostage was taken.

Some of the money was diverted (by Lt Col Oliver North*, then serving with the National Security Council) into funding the Contra rebel movement in armed conflict with the socialist Sandinista government of Nicaragua.

The withholding and destruction of masses of documents by the administration meant that Reagan himself was never held directly responsible for this complicated web of deceit.

And so who paid the price for 'Irangate'? Nobody, long term. In the final days of his presidency, George H.W. Bush, who had been vice-president at the time, issued pardons to one and all.

---

* *In 2018 he was appointed president of the National Rifle Association.*

Vox pops

Nothing disturbs the settled ruling classes more than an uncouth, disrespectful character who shoulders his way to the forefront of national politics claiming to speak for the downtrodden masses – and finds them cheering him to the rafters.

Populism's Exhibit A is Andrew Jackson, the war hero dubbed 'Old Hickory' by admirers who thought him as tough as the notoriously hard timber. He was the man of the people.

The 1828 US election was a re-match against an opponent who had narrowly defeated him four years earlier. This was John Quincy Adams, a scholar, diplomat and lawyer whose father had been one of the Founding Fathers and the new country's second president. As far as Jackson was concerned, John Quincy was the embodiment of a self-serving, privileged old guard. He was one of the elite.

It turned out to be a vicious, verbal mud-slinging campaign – the Era of Good Feelings was well and truly over!

The Log Cabin Election

William Henry Harrison's promoters in the 1840 election knew how to touch the populist nerve by presenting him as the 'common man' – although he had actually been born in a southern mansion.

In their shameless image-making marketing campaign, silk banners displayed an image of 'Old Tippecanoe' (a nickname from one of his military exploits in the war of 1812) standing in front of a log cabin alongside a cask of cider – a beverage liberally dispensed at his public meetings.

His PR team wrote campaign songs and published their own newspapers.* You could buy 'Tippecanoe shaving soap – or log-cabin emollient'; miniature log cabins; ceramic dishes depicting the candidate's 'modest' farm; and hairbrushes with his picture on them.

The result was a sharp increase in voter turnout – and the triumph of Harrison's Whigs after twelve years of Democrat rule.

* *Including* The Log Cabin, *published by Horace Greeley, who the following year would found the forerunner of today's* New York Herald Tribune.

Jackson's pitch was that Adams and his administration were corrupt and ignored 'the voice of the people'.

Although he was constantly pilloried for his slave trading, his marital mix-up, his duelling, his impulsive military behaviour (one leaflet displayed coffins to represent executed deserters) and his callous treatment of Native Americans, none of this seemed to matter.

He had not, ran a supportive newspaper editorial, 'been educated at foreign courts and reared on sweetmeats from the tables of kings and princes'.

That's what counted!

Ignoring the issues of the day, he concentrated on promoting his image, erecting large hickory poles in town squares and attaching smaller ones to church steeples and steamboats.

He won by a landslide, establishing his 'common man' philosophy for a generation— and introducing a 'spoils system' that gave top civil service jobs to his friends and allies.

On Jackson's inauguration day crowds flocked to the White House in wild celebration – and trashed it.

Trumped

Once installed in the Oval Office, Donald Trump (populism's Exhibit B) installed a portrait of Jackson on the wall and paid a tribute visit to the Hermitage, his mansion in Tennessee. Old Hickory was to be his talisman.

There were, it should be said, many differences between the two:

- Jackson was born in poverty, whereas Trump inherited a fortune worth around $140m (£100m) in today's terms from his father

- Jackson was a renowned military leader, whereas Trump avoided the draft during the Vietnam War

- Jackson was a career politician, whereas Trump had never run for office before

But this just helps us tick off a few of the things that don't matter when a 'man of the people' persuades millions to vote for him.

Books

Sales of George Orwell's 1984 soared in America after Donald Trump's election, but two home-grown novels are must-reads for anyone worried (or excited) by populist politics.

Sinclair Lewis's *It Can't Happen Here* was published in 1935, during the rise of Hitler, and charts the rise of the demagogue 'Buzz' Windrip, who is elected US President on a programme of patriotism and traditional values. Windrip quickly establishes a cruel totalitarian rule, revealing the weakness of the nation's democratic safeguards.

In his award-winning *The Plot Against America*, published in 2004, Philip Roth imagines that Franklin D. Roosevelt was defeated in the 1940 presidential campaign by the famous aviator Charles Lindbergh – in real life a spokesman for the America First Party who praised Hitler and criticised 'the Jewish race' for attempting to involve the US in the Second World War. In Roth's alternative history Lindbergh signs a treaty with Nazi Germany and relocates Jewish families to the western states, stirring a latent antisemitism which erupts in rioting and bloodshed. Now read on ...

Here's an abbreviated list of the accusations Trump faced,* both during his campaign and once he had begun to govern.

- He was an uncouth rabble-rouser, constantly referring to his Democrat rival as 'Crooked Hillary' and inciting crowds at his rallies to yell 'Lock her up!'

- He was a racist, manipulating events to stir up feelings against Muslims and immigrants

- He was a womaniser and a sexist, who had many affairs (most of them denied) and talked about 'grabbing women by the pussy'

- He was a danger to the Constitution, attacking 'Obama judges' for decisions he didn't like and the media for presenting 'fake news'

- He was a danger internationally, cozying up to dictators and shredding agreements – among them measures to protect the world from the consequences of global warming

---

* *More serious potentially than public opprobrium was an investigation by special counsel Robert Mueller into alleged Russian interference in the 2016 election with the collusion of the Trump campaign.*

'I think if this country gets any kinder or gentler it's literally going to cease to exist.'

Donald Trump, interviewed in Playboy *magazine*

- He was a compulsive liar, even denying his own previous statements when it suited him

- He was a braggart, turning every issue towards himself and presenting his failures as glorious successes

Promising to 'drain the swamp' of the Washington and New York elite, he harnessed the power of the internet by firing off wildly intemperate tweets to his followers in the middle of the night – often to the despair of his own inner circle.

What did his supporters say to all this?

- He tells it like it is, even if we don't agree with everything he says and does

- He puts America First (one of his campaign slogans)

- He'll Make America Great Again (another of his slogans)

It's a short list and it lacks detail, but that's the point: the skill of the populist politico lies in triggering a positive gut reaction in his followers – and 'The Donald' had proved himself a master in pushing those buttons.

Few commentators, whether for him or against, would contest Donald Trump's reputation as the greatest maverick ever to occupy the White House.

In 2017 more than 60,000 mental health professionals went further, signing a petition that claimed his erratic behaviour betrayed 'a serious mental illness' which should rule him out of the job.

When he lost the House of Representatives to the Democrats in the 2018 mid-term elections ('our Big Victory', he typically acclaimed on Twitter), the scene was set for two further years of political turbulence, its impact to be experienced not only in America itself but all over the nervously waiting world.

It was, to coin a phrase, A Very Peculiar Presidency.

What they did afterwards

While some slipped into a quiet retirement, other presidents found ways to stay busy...

• Thomas Jefferson founded the University of Virginia. He designed its buildings, planned its curriculum and served as its first rector when it opened in 1825.

• John Quincy Adams won a seat in the House of Representatives (the only former president to do so) and served for another 18 years until his death.

• Rutherford B. Hayes campaigned vigorously for federal education subsidies, advocated better conditions in prisons and railed against the gap between rich and poor. 'Excessive wealth in the hands of the few,' he wrote, 'means extreme poverty, ignorance, vice and wretchedness as the lot of the many.'

• Theodore Roosevelt gave his name to teddy bears after news of his sparing of a sick black bear on a hunting trip in 1902 spread around the world. Once retired he was *unsparing*. In 1909 he went on safari to eastern Africa with his son and 200 porters – and returned with a proud list of 512 wild animals killed.

• In 1921, eight years after leaving office, William Taft was appointed Chief Justice, the only ex-president to hold the post. Worried about his health, he walked the 4.8km (three miles) to and from work each day, and after his death his regular crossing of Rock Creek, Connecticut, was named the Taft Bridge.

• Herbert Hoover organised the shipment of 40,000 tons of food from the United States to millions of starving German children after the end of the Second World War through the *Hooverspeisung* initiative. The lightest of the many books he wrote during his retirement was *Fishing for Fun – and to Wash Your Soul,* his declared philosophy a succinct take on the Declaration of Independence: 'All men are equal before fish.'

• Jimmy Carter's single term isn't generally regarded as a great success, but his attempts to bring peace to troubled areas of the world prefigured what he would do later. In 1982 he founded the Carter Center to promote and expand human rights, and he travelled widely to conduct peace negotiations and on campaigns to prevent and eradicate diseases in developing nations. In 2002 he was awarded the Nobel Peace Prize – the only president to receive it after leaving office.

Glossary

brevet An honorary military title, raising an officer to a higher rank for outstanding service, but without an increase in pay.

caucus A meeting at which members of a political party meet to choose their preferred presidential candidate.

faithless elector A member of the Electoral College who breaks a pledge to vote for a particular candidate.

hanging chad A circle of paper that fails to separate from a punched ballot form, so making it null and void.

Manifest Destiny Coined in 1845, the notion that the US should expand its territory across North America.

pyrrhic victory A triumph so wounding to the winner that it amounts to a defeat.

presidential primary An election in which parties in each state make the choice of their preferred candidate in the coming national campaign. In some states this is achieved by a *caucus* or a combination of the two.

spoils system First introduced by Andrew Jackson, and prevalent in the US until reforms in 1883, the practice of giving jobs in the civil service to friends and supporters rather than filling them on merit.

veto A president's power to refuse the passing of a bill into law. Only a two-thirds vote in Congress can overturn it.

Presidents timeline

1789 George Washington takes office as the first US president; Bill of Rights passed.

1791 The Whiskey Rebellion, later put down by Washington.

1799 John Fries's Rebellion.

1800 White House first occupied, by John Adams; *Life of George Washington* published by Parson Weems.

1801 Jefferson sends fleet against Barbary pirates in the Mediterranean.

1803 The Louisiana Purchase vastly expands US territory.

1804 Lewis and Clark expedition to the Pacific.

1806 Andrew Jackson kills Charles Dickinson in a duel, and is himself wounded; Jefferson's grandson James is the first baby to be born in the White House.

1812 Start of war with Britain.

1814 The British burn down the White House.

1815 Jackson defeats British at Battle of New Orleans.

1823 Monroe Doctrine declared (although not so named until 1850)

1825 Thomas Jefferson founds University of Virginia.

1826 Jefferson and John Adams die on the same day.

1828 Democratic-Republican Party formed, forerunner of today's Democrats.

1830 Jackson's Indian Removal Act drives Native Americans west of the Mississippi.

1841 Death in office of William Henry Harrison.

1846–48 Mexican American War.

1850 Death in office of Zachary Taylor.

1854 Republican Party formed.

1859 South Carolina is the first state to secede from the Union (December).

1860 Breakaway Confederate States of America formed.

1861–65 American Civil War.

1863 Lincoln's Emancipation Proclamation and Gettysburg Address.

1865 Confederate forces surrender at Appomattox; Slavery is abolished under the 13th Amendment; Lincoln is assassinated and Johnson becomes president.

1865 Civil Rights Act makes everyone born in the US a citizen. (Confirmed in 14th Amendment three years later).

1867 Johnson administration buys Alaska from the Russian Empire.

1868 Andrew Johnson is impeached.

1872 Victoria Woodhull is the first woman to run for president.

1881 Assassination of James Garfield.

1898 Spanish-American War.

1901 Assassination of William McKinley; Theodore Roosevelt adds West Wing to the White House.

1906 Theodore Roosevelt awarded Nobel Peace Prize.

1912 Theodore Roosevelt is shot, but survives.

1915 *Birth of a Nation* is the first film ever shown in the White House.

1919 Woodrow Wilson signs Treaty of Versailles after the end of the First World War; he is awarded the Nobel Peace Prize.

1921 Beginning of Teapot Dome scandal.

1923 Death in office of Warren Harding.

1932 Franklin D. Roosevelt promotes New Deal during his election campaign.

1941 Completion of Mount Rushmore sculptures.

1945 Death in office of Franklin D. Roosevelt; Truman orders atom bomb to be dropped on Hiroshima.

1948 Truman's executive order ends racial segregation in the military.

1957 Eisenhower's Civil Rights Act protects black Americans' right to vote; black children prevented from enrolling in school at Little Rock, Arkansas.

1962 Kennedy faces Cuban missile crisis.

1963 Violent suppression of protests against racial segregation in Alabama; assassination of John F. Kennedy.

1964 Johnson's Civil Rights Act outlaws segregation in all public places.

1965 Johnson orders troops into Vietnam.

1972 Nixon visits China, bringing a thaw in relations; break-in at Democrats' headquarters in Washington is the beginning of the Watergate scandal.

1974 Nixon resigns to avoid impeachment.

1993 Ronald Reagan is shot, but survives.

1998 Bill Clinton is impeached.

2001 George W. Bush announces 'War on Terror' after the September 11th al-Qaeda attack that kills around 3,000 Americans.

2002 Jimmy Carter is awarded the Nobel Peace Prize.

2009 Barack Obama becomes the first black president and is awarded the Nobel Peace Prize.

2017 Donald Trump is the first president with no political or military experience.

Index

Some other
Very Peculiar Histories™

The Blitz
David Arscott
ISBN: 978-1-907184-18-5

Castles
Jacqueline Morley
ISBN: 978-1-907184-48-2

Charles Dickens
Fiona Macdonald
ISBN: 978-1-908177-15-5

Golf
David Arscott
ISBN: 978-1-907184-75-8

Great Britons
Ian Graham
ISBN: 978-1-907184-59-8

Ireland
Jim Pipe
ISBN: 978-1-905638-98-7

Kings & Queens
Antony Mason
ISBN: 978-1-906714-77-2

London
Jim Pipe
ISBN: 978-1-907184-26-0

Scotland
Fiona Macdonald

Vol. 1: From ancient times
to Robert the Bruce
ISBN: 978-1-906370-91-6

Vol. 2: From the Stewarts
to modern Scotland
ISBN: 978-1-906714-79-6

Wales
Rupert Matthews
ISBN: 978-1-907184-19-2

Whisky
Fiona Macdonald
ISBN: 978-1-907184-76-5

For the full list, visit
www.salariya.com